AF799876

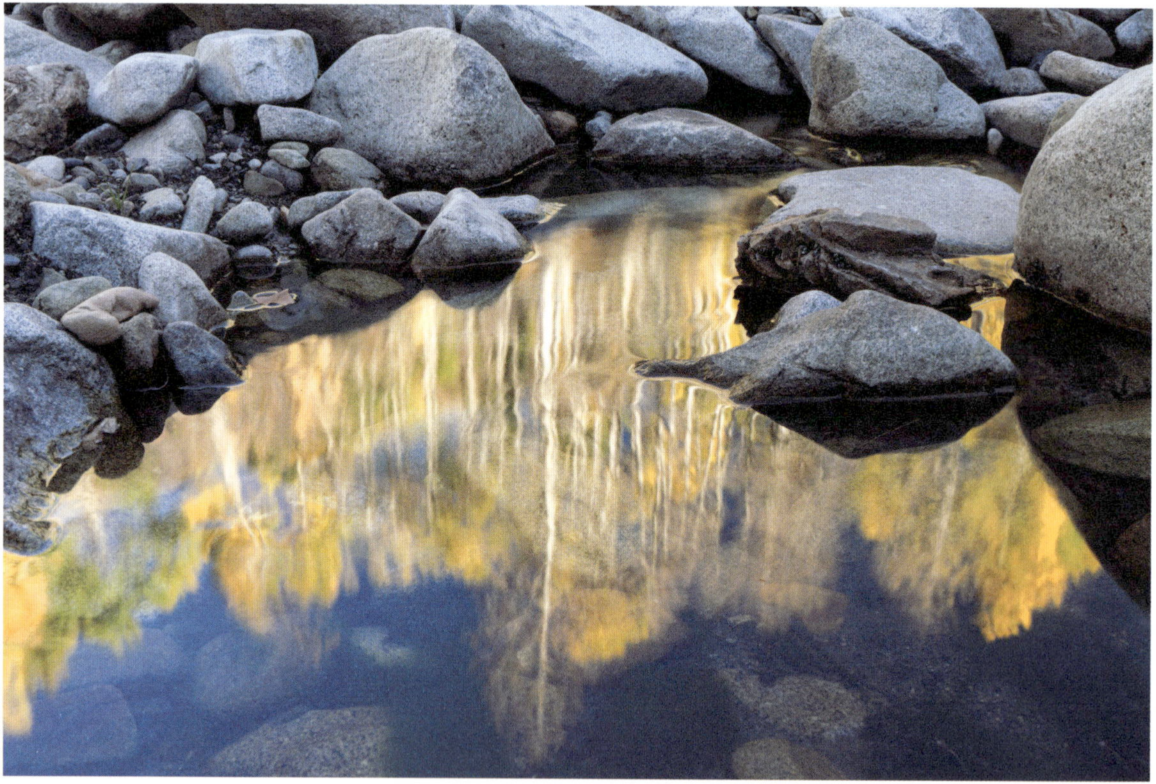

# Illuminating Nature

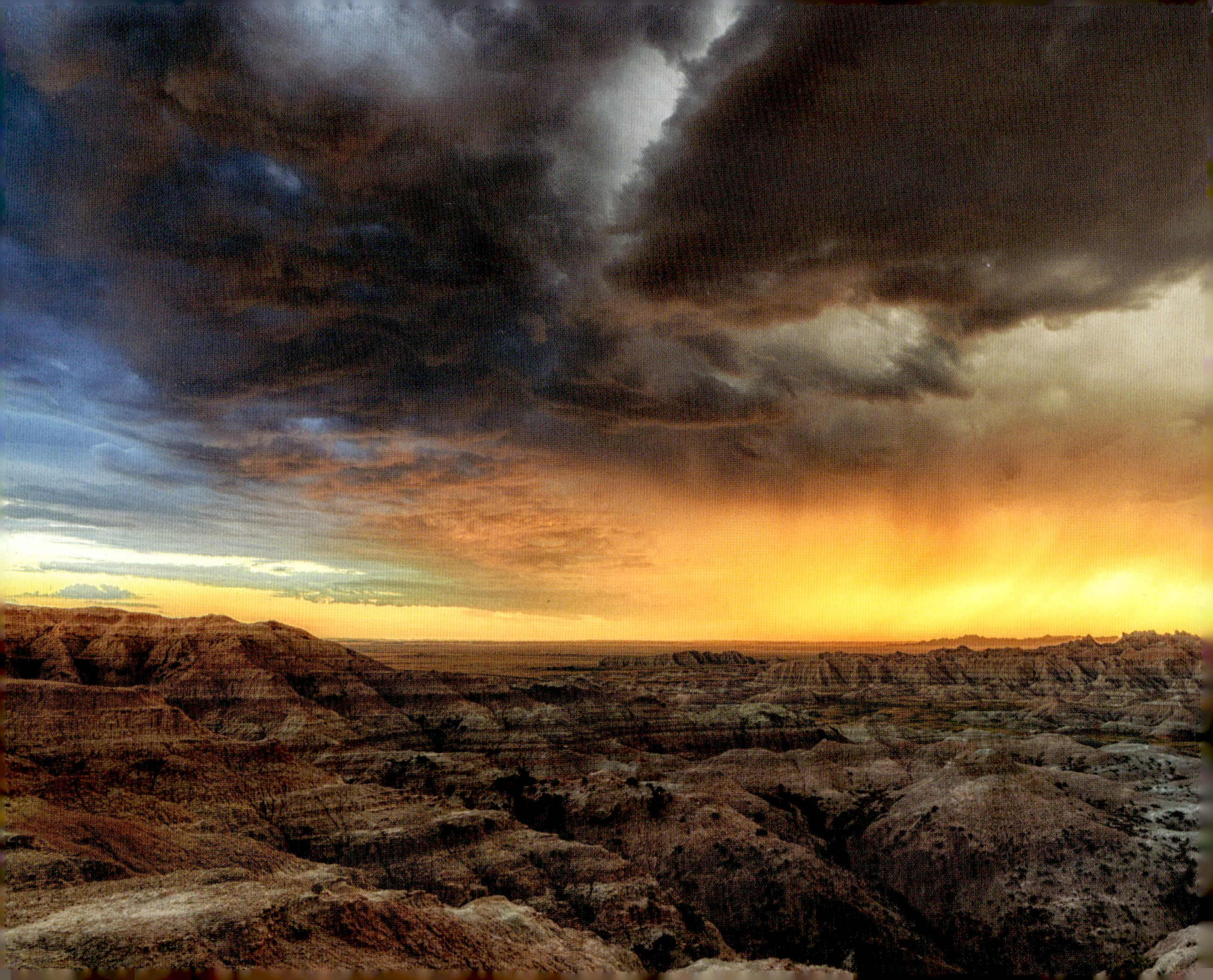

# Illuminating Nature

CHASING LIGHT ACROSS THE LANDSCAPE

Jon Reynolds

**Countryman Press**

*An Imprint of W. W. Norton & Company*
*Independent Publishers Since 1923*

Copyright © 2024 by Jon Reynolds

All rights reserved
Printed in China

For information about permission to reproduce selections from this book, write to
Permissions, Countryman Press, 500 Fifth Avenue, New York, NY 10110

For information about special discounts for bulk purchases, please contact
W. W. Norton Special Sales at specialsales@wwnorton.com or 800-233-4830

Manufacturing by RRD Asia
Book design by Allison Chi
Production manager: Devon Zahn

Countryman Press
www.countrymanpress.com

An imprint of W. W. Norton & Company, Inc.
500 Fifth Avenue, New York, NY 10110
www.wwnorton.com

978-1-68268-945-5

10 9 8 7 6 5 4 3 2 1

Previous: *Badlands National Park, South Dakota*
Right: *Lake Irwin, Gunnison National Forest, Colorado*

For Jen

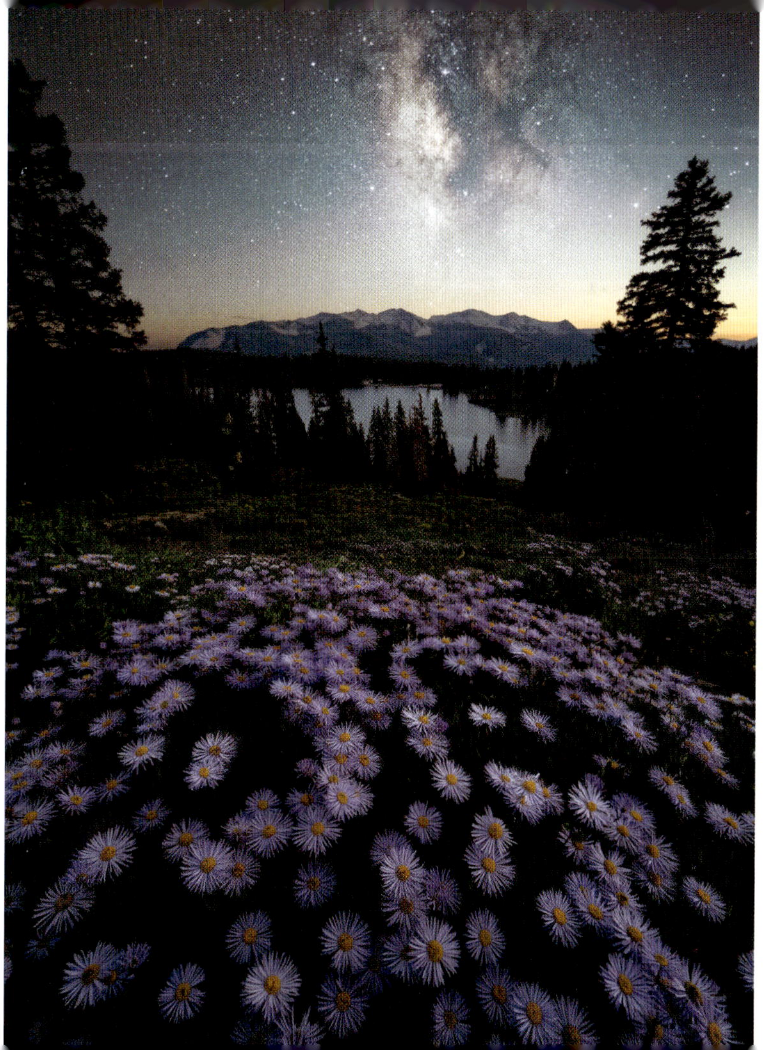

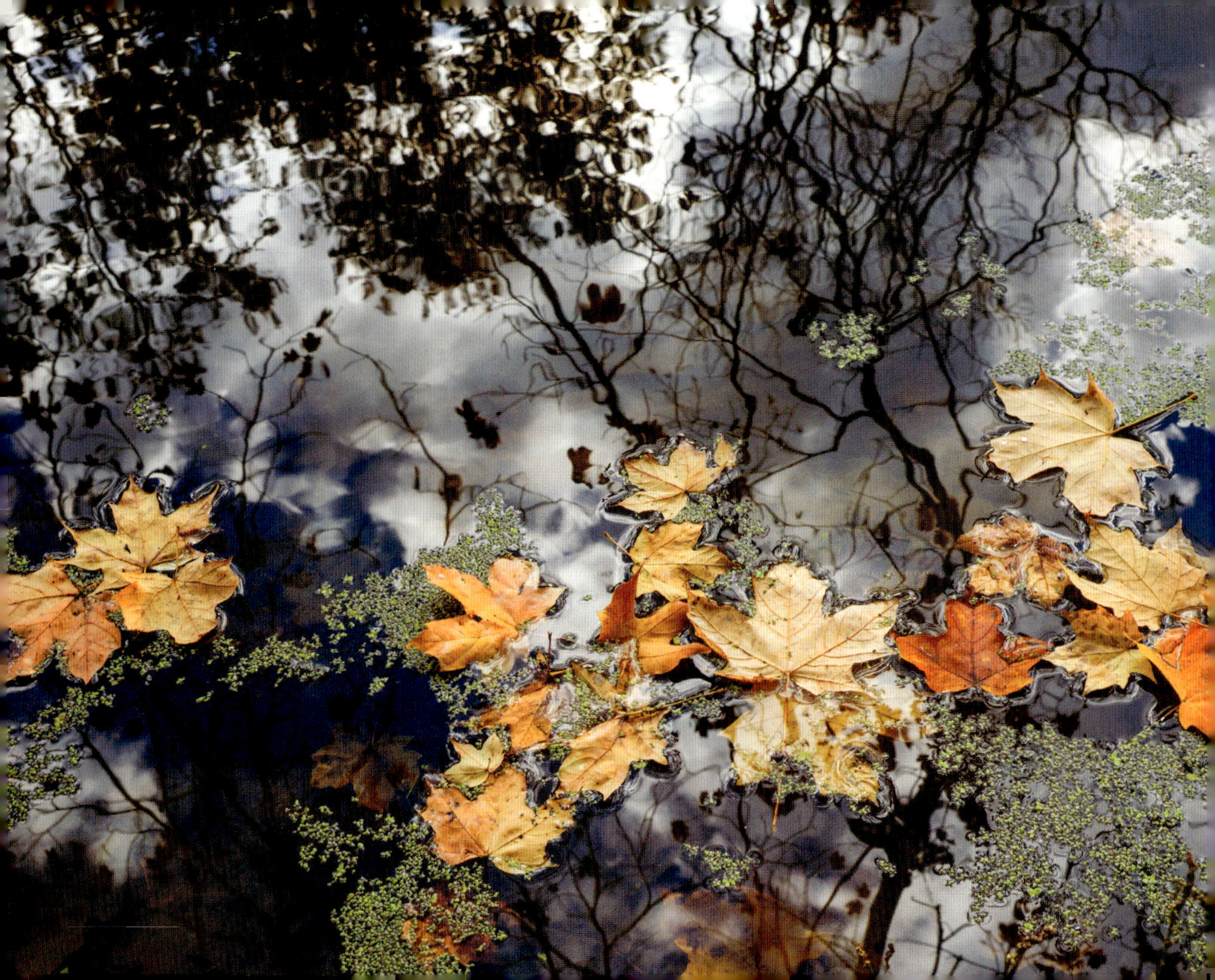

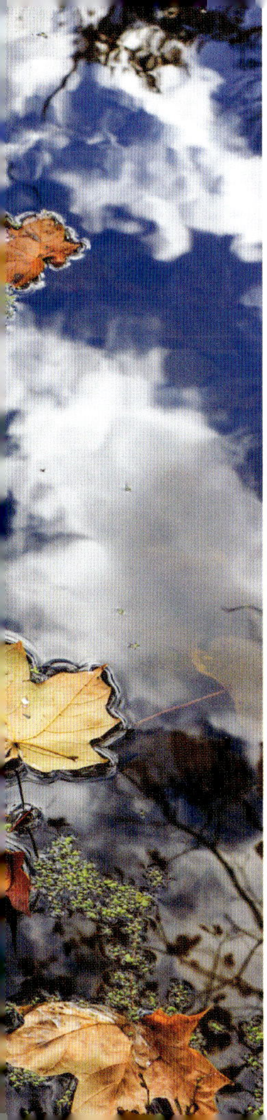

# Contents



*Erlanger, Kentucky*

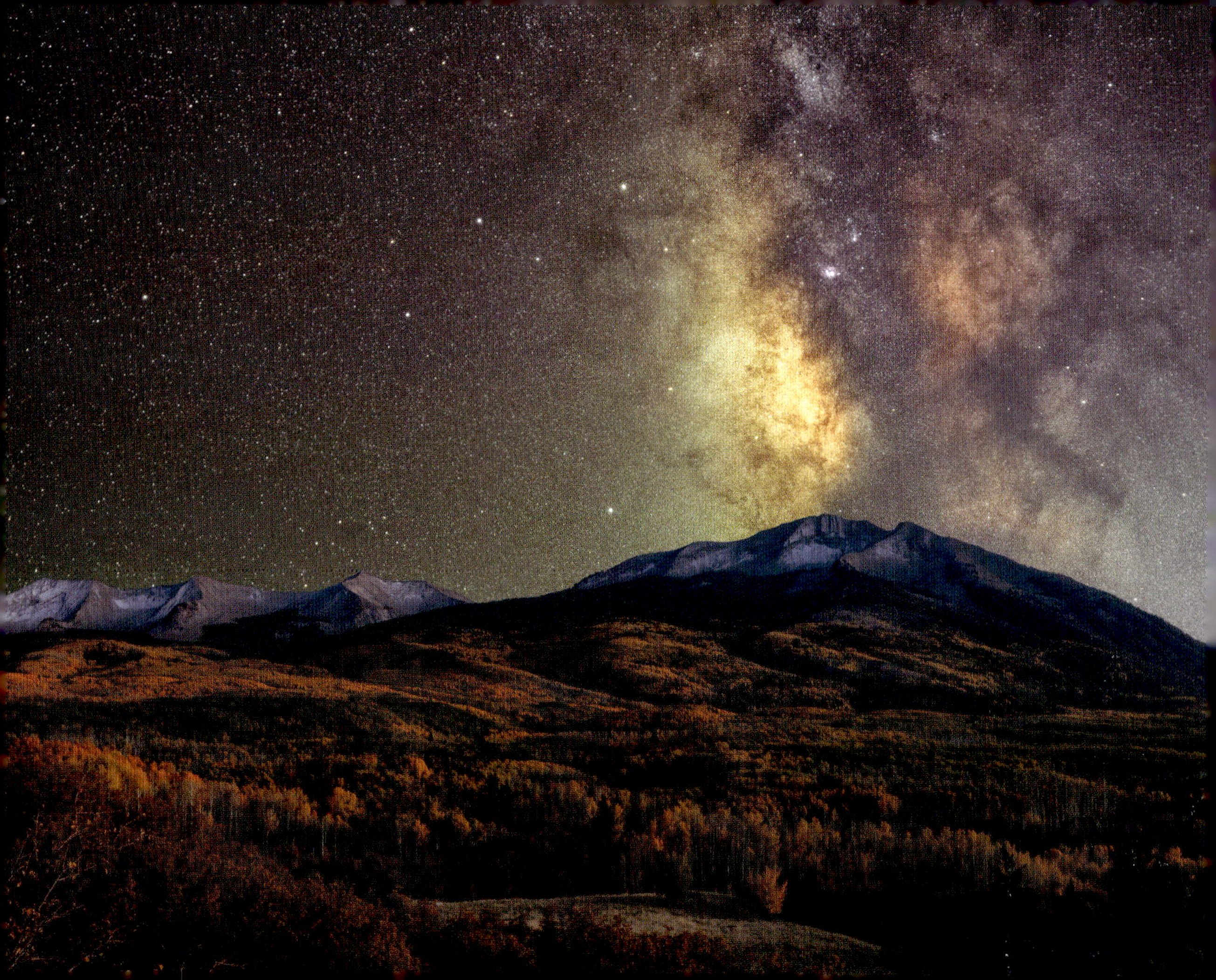

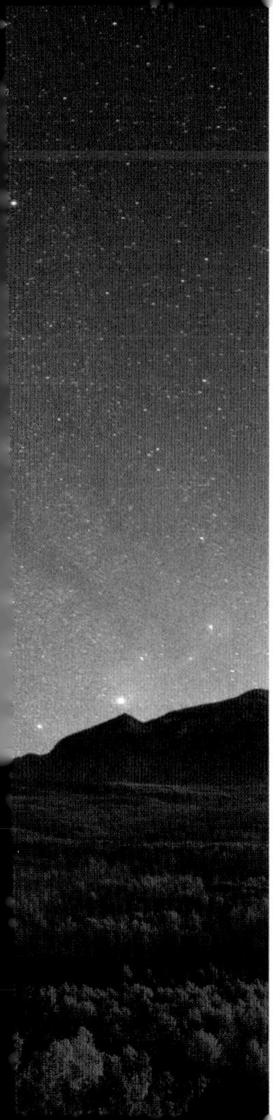

# Introduction

It was early September 2012 when I noticed the gathering of geese in the pond adjacent to my workplace. I would occasionally see the striking V patterns of the migratory flocks overhead while going about my day. "Why not bring my camera and try to get a picture?" I thought. The camera had been gathering dust in my closet since I bought it the year before to take on a trip.

The following morning, I pulled up next to the pond, grabbed my gear, slammed the door, and stomped over to the water's edge. Suddenly, a frenzy of flapping and splashing began, followed by a churning pool of ripples where the flock of geese had just been swimming. I hadn't even removed my camera from the bag. "Oh," I thought as I dejectedly returned to the car, "I have to be quiet next time!"

Every day for the next four months the piercing squawks of ascending geese filled the morning air, followed by the desperate

*Kebler Pass, Gunnison National Forest, Colorado*

cries of a frustrated hobbyist. Finally, one clear, frigid December morning, frustration turned to exultation: a clear image of the geese, frozen in flight in the warming sunrise of early winter.

Eleven years and countless lost lens caps later, I am still chasing the thrill of that moment. It has led me to hike down mountain passes in Colorado on golden fall afternoons, to trudge across the Dakota Badlands in icy winters, to follow glittering streams deep in the sun-dappled woods of West Virginia, Tennessee, and North Carolina. It has led me from sunrises on the coast of Maine to starry nights in New Mexico to moonsets and solar eclipses in Utah.

This short volume documents the ongoing pursuit. Although I think photographs should speak for themselves, I have shared some anecdotes, insights, and quotations that have inspired me and serve as written analogues to the visual images included herein. One of those quotations is from Ralph Waldo Emerson, to whom I will give the final word here. Emerson observed that when someone spends time seeking out the healing qualities of nature, "He finds himself. The health of the eye seems to demand a horizon. We are never tired, so long as we can see far enough."

# The Photographs

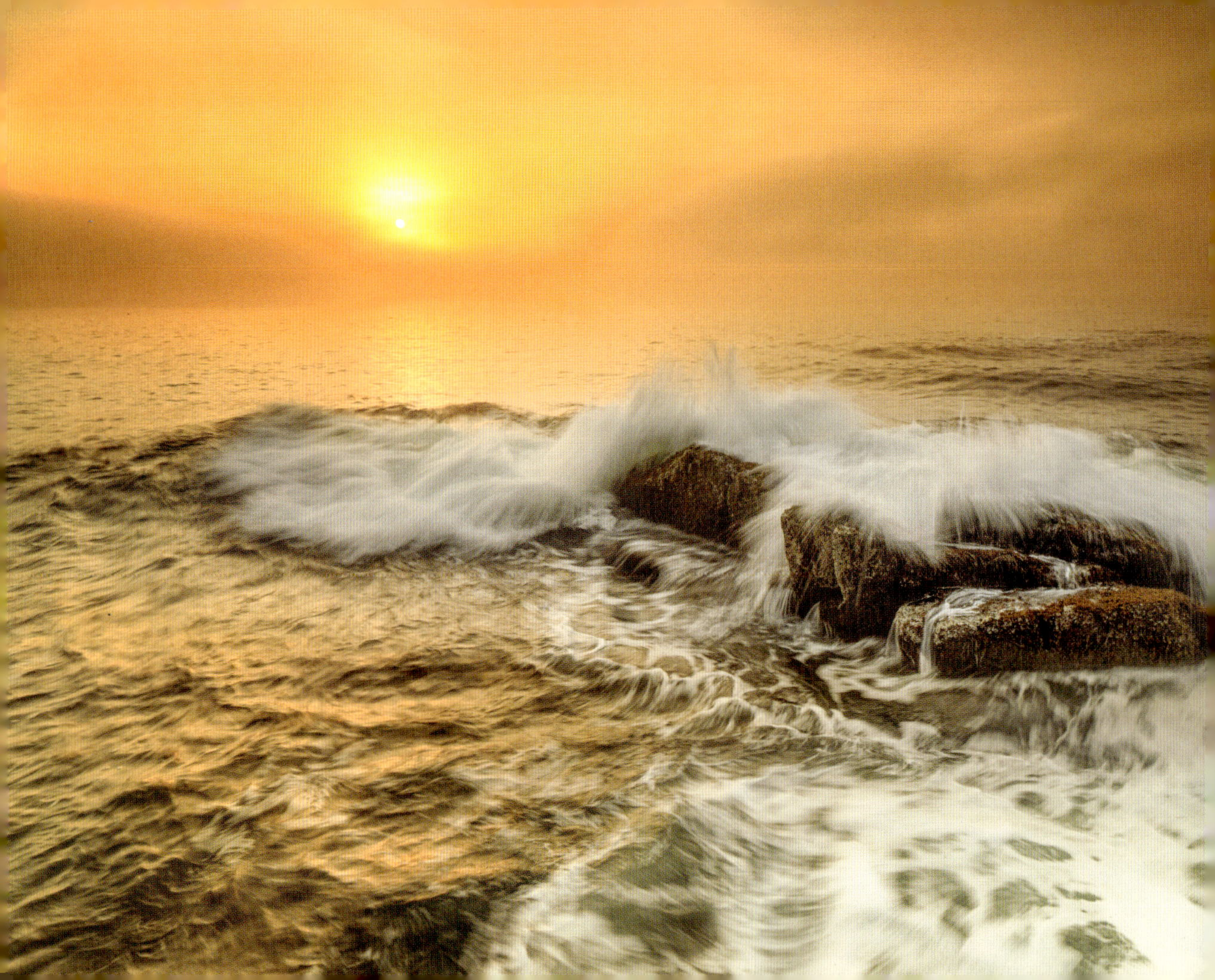

*At dawn, the familiar names of famous places don't much matter. . . . You need pay attention only to the forms of this landscape emerging from night, a natural reciprocity of land and water shaped by climate and honed by weather, attended by the casual genius of sea level expressing itself as a restless edge of tide.*

—CHRISTOPHER CAMUTO, *TIME AND TIDE IN ACADIA*

*Acadia National Park, Maine*

I arrived at Boulder Beach in Maine's Acadia National Park at 3:30 a.m. for sunrise, full of excitement. As I carefully descended the slippery slabs of sloping granite, I was met with an all-encompassing fog, deafening surf, and an army of midges. In vain I searched for the east, but in the endless darkness I lost all sense of direction.

**4:54 a.m.:** Sunrise. My deteriorating enthusiasm further eroded as the shroud of fog selfishly claimed the horizon and merged with the sea to form a dull gray void. The bare edges of a rocky outcropping began to emerge amid the crashing waves of high tide.

**5:15 a.m.:** A glimmer of light began to appear in the distance.

**5:29 a.m.:** A blaze of orange splashed across the sky and an exultant smile spread across my midge-bitten face.

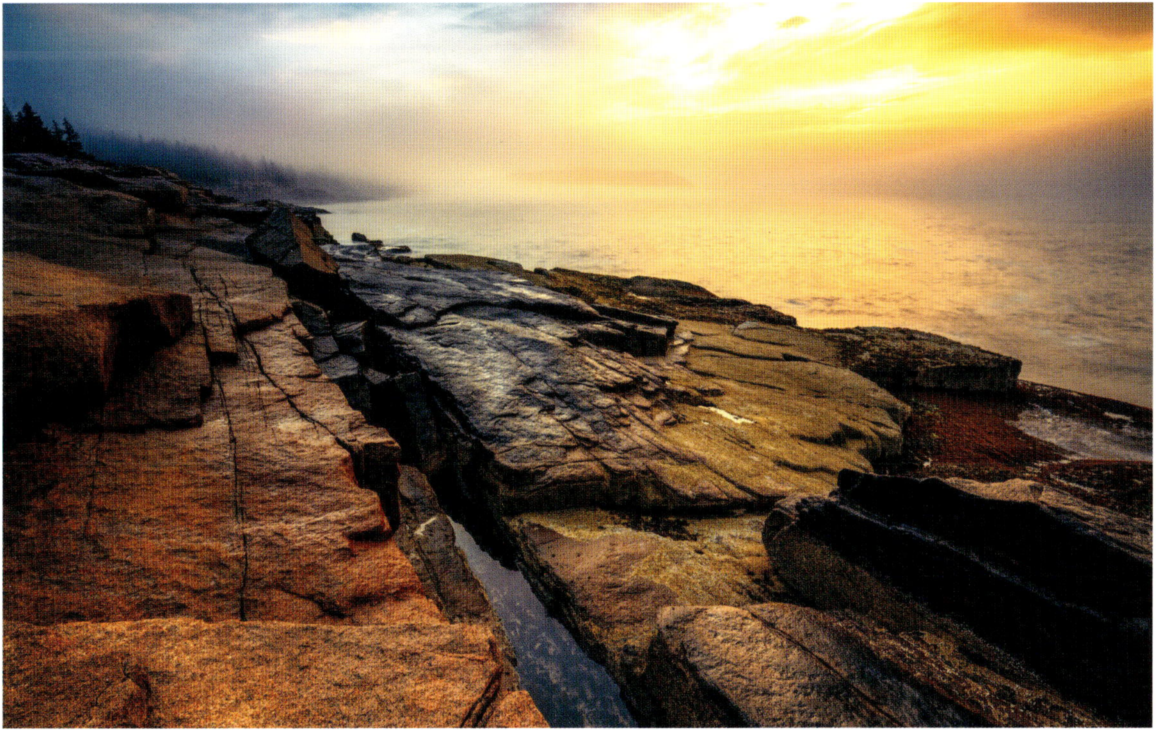

*Acadia National Park, Maine*

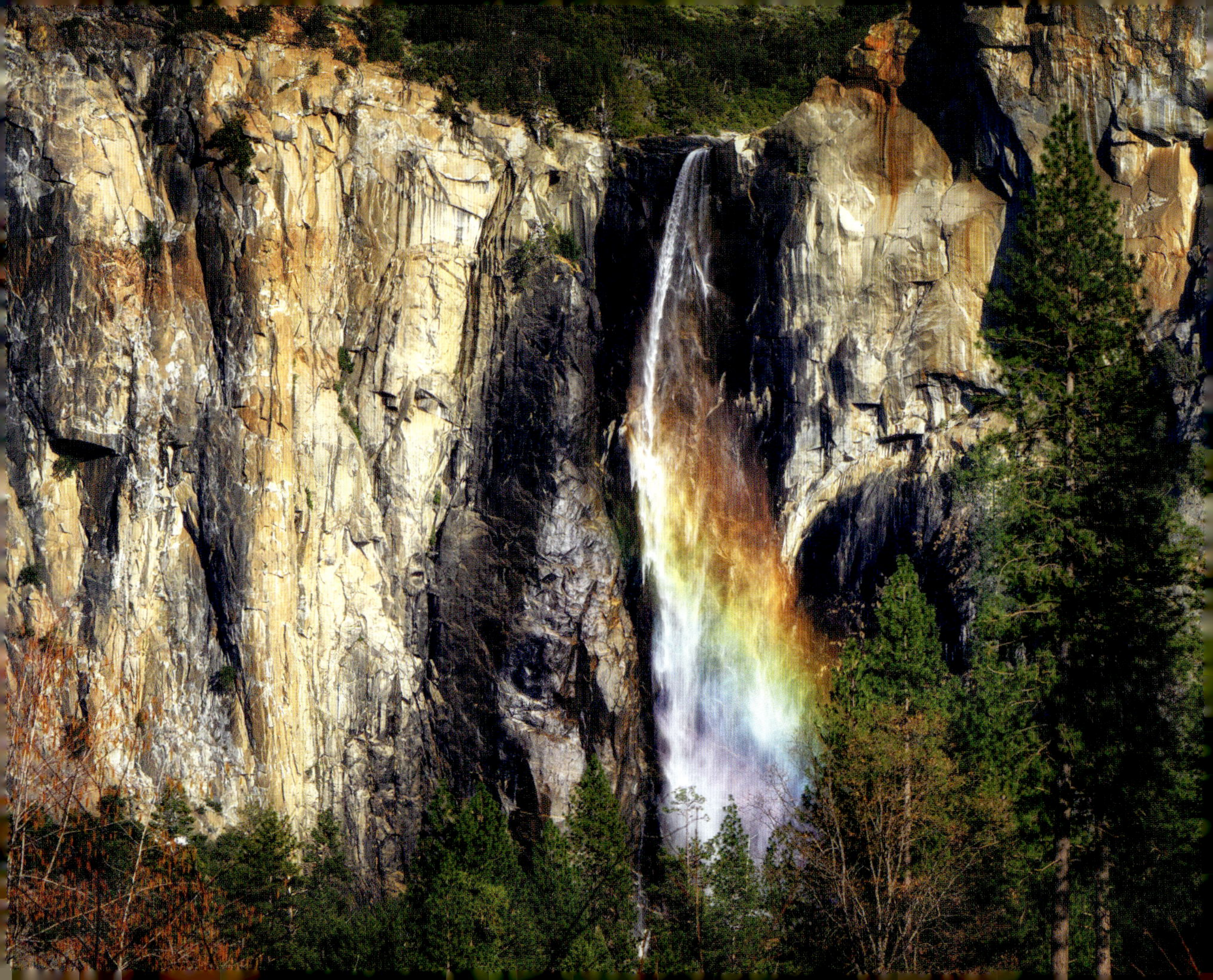

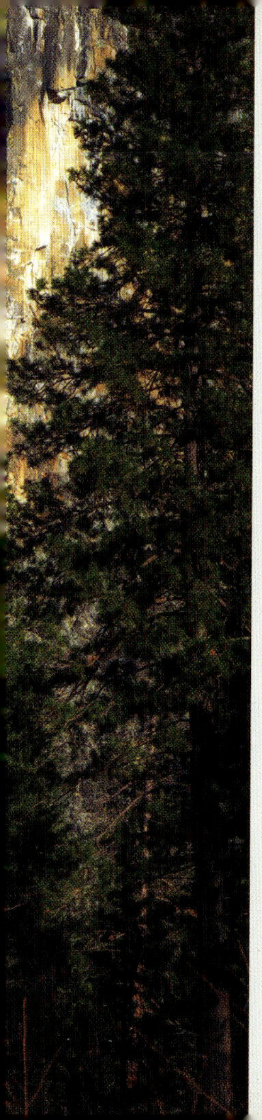

*The external world has nothing but shapes, but we see form, weight, balance, and values. We also see and feel more esoteric and intangible things. I want to take photographs that have all that in them. . . . A more realistic simple snapshot captures the image but misses everything else. I want a picture to reflect not only the forms but what I had seen and felt at the moment of exposure.*

—ANSEL ADAMS

*Bridalveil Fall, Yosemite National Park, California*

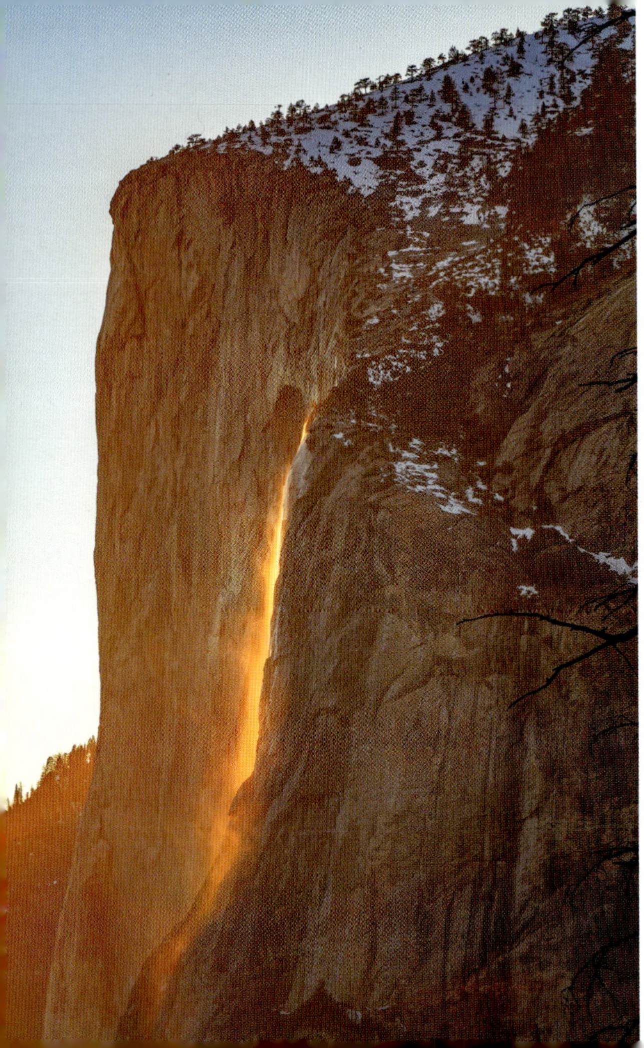
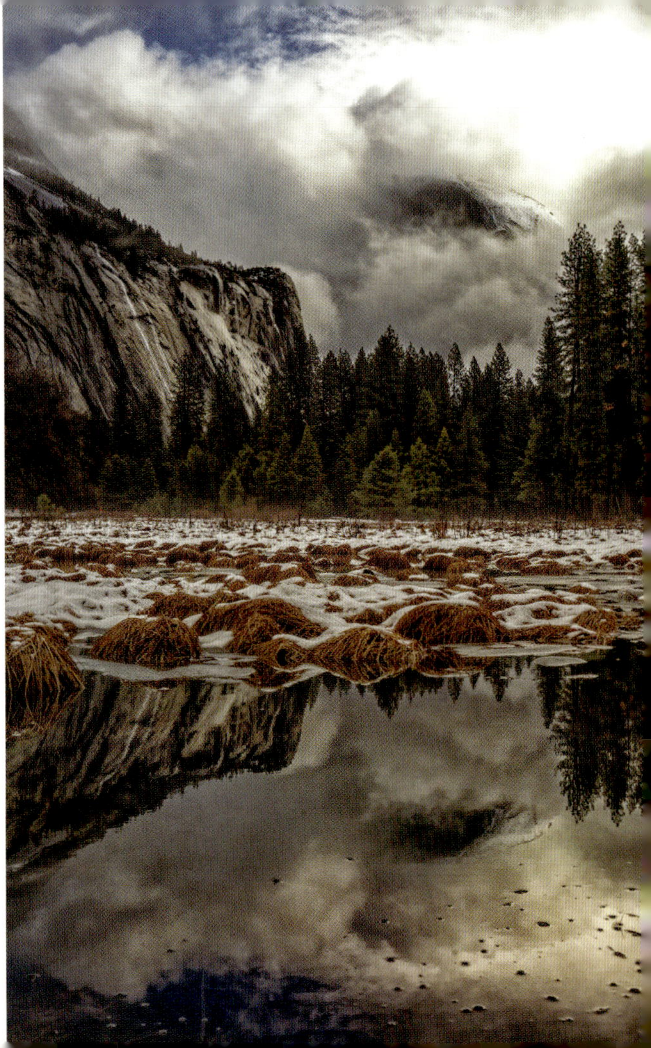

How do you get a unique shot of the most photographed icons of the United States? The short answer is you can't. Instead you dismiss the weight of expectations and focus on the task at hand. How does the subject affect *you*? How does the interplay of light and shadow appear at the time *you* are there, not in the iconic images of Ansel Adams or a thousand photographers on social media? Are *you* willing to get out of bed before the sun rises and stay long after the sun sets, to wait until clouds pass or arrive? In the end, you take pictures for yourself. The faster you chase perfection, the faster it runs away from you.

Left: *Firefall at Horsetail Falls, Yosemite National Park, California*
Right: *Half Dome, Yosemite National Park, California*

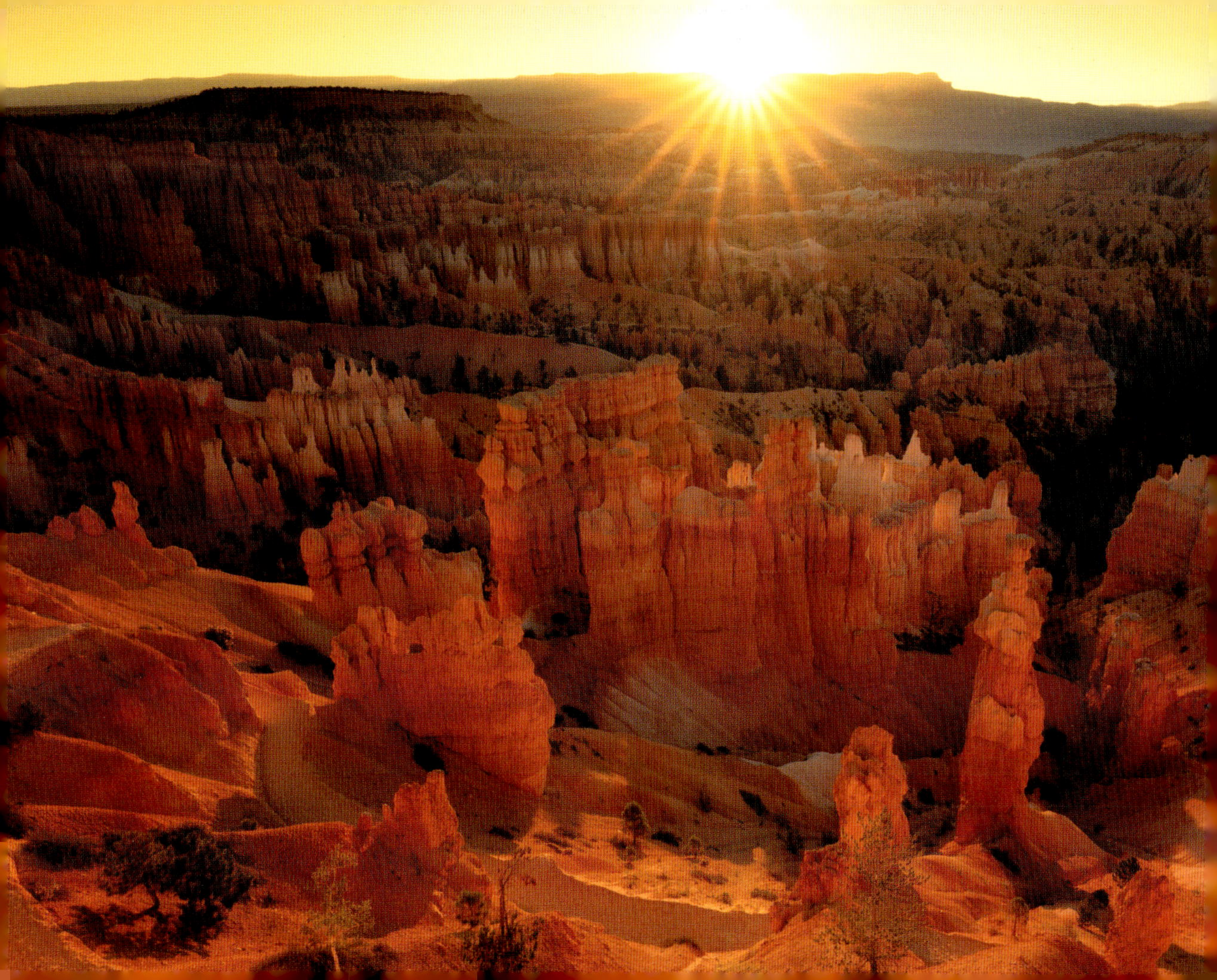

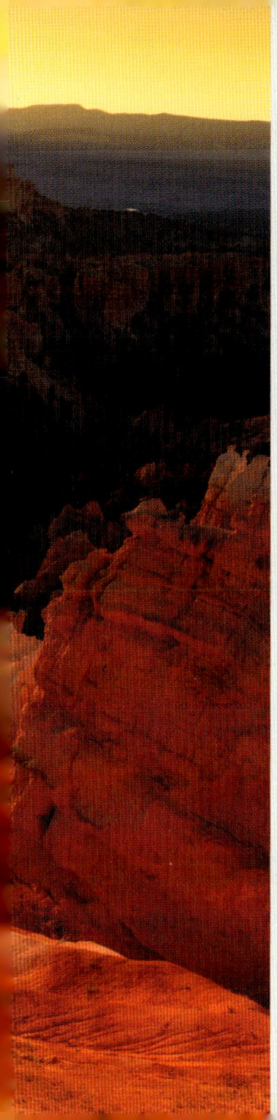

*Tell me, what is it you plan to do*
*with your one wild and precious life?*

—MARY OLIVER, "THE SUMMER DAY"

*Bryce Canyon National Park, Utah*

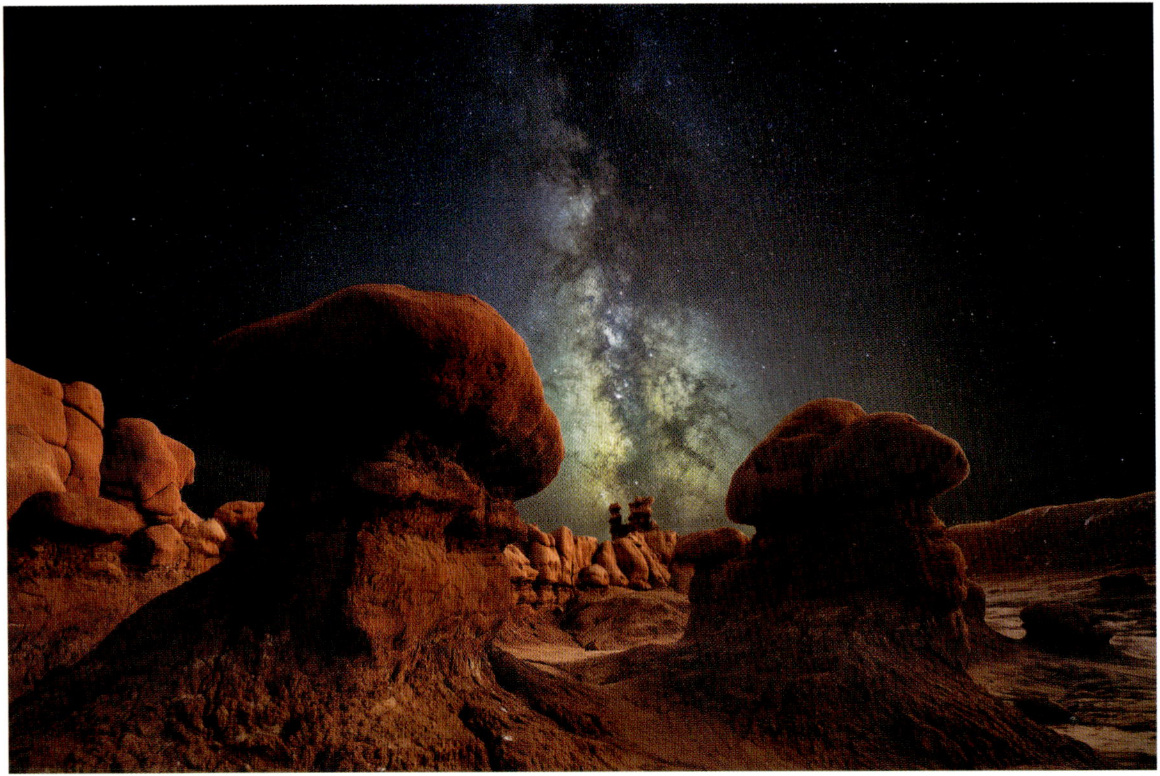

*Goblin Valley State Park, Utah*

A couple of days before a trip, a friend commented that he didn't have the time or patience to be a photographer. "I just want to take a pic with my phone and move on," he said. I sympathized with him, but countered with the cliché that anything worth doing is worth waiting for. He grinned. "Then I'll just wait for you to do it!"

Watching the sun's last stretch of light slip away and the mushroom-shaped hoodoos cast longer and longer shadows across the lunar-like landscape of Goblin Valley State Park, I thought about that conversation. As the blue twilight sky slowly turned into a starry canvas, I began to tally my time: thirty hours to drive here, three or so hours to scout locations. In one hour the galactic center of the Milky Way would appear along the horizon and then sink like a ship into the pitch-black sea of night. I could move on after that. Or in twenty hours, I could do it all again.

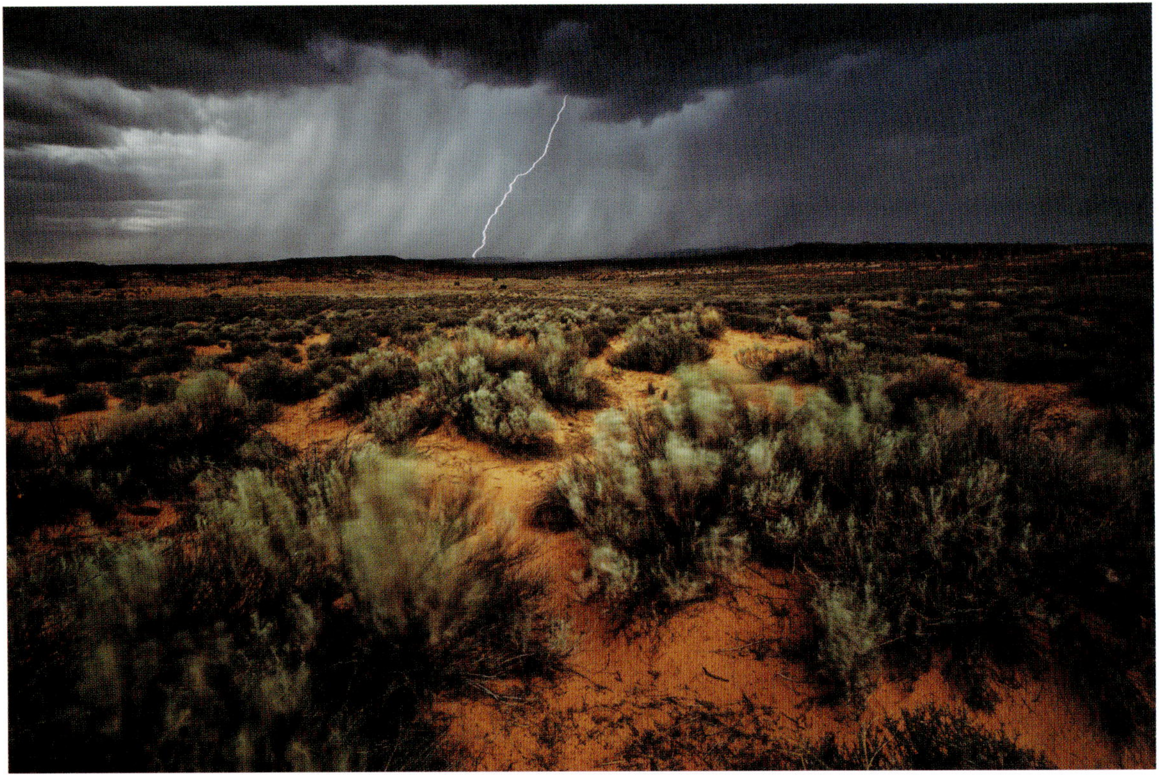

Left and right: *Arches National Park, Utah*

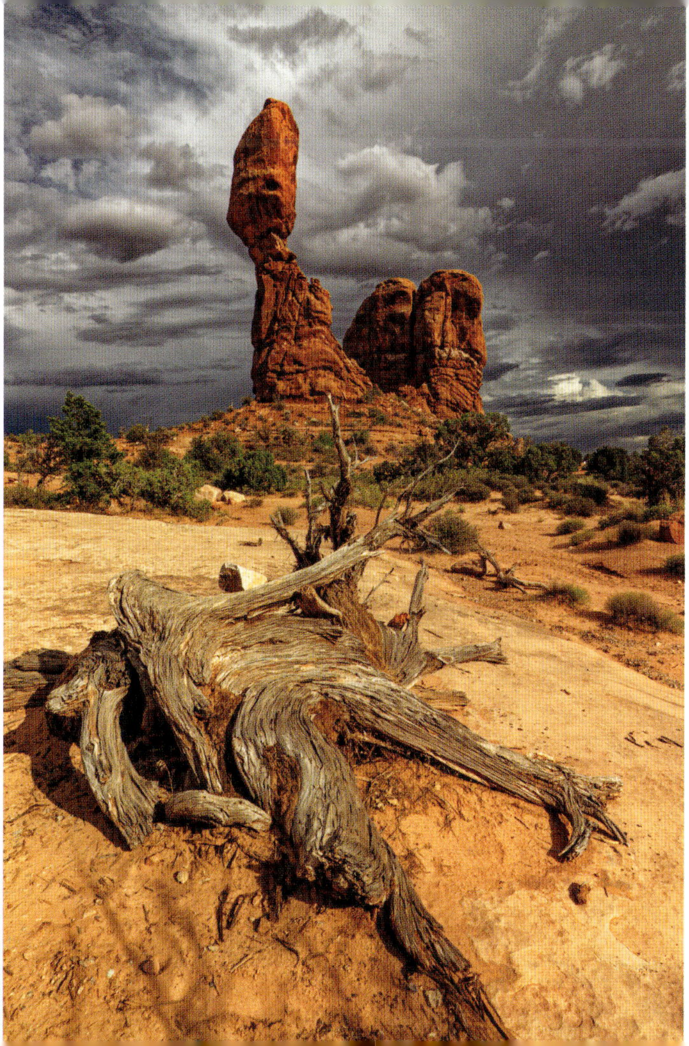

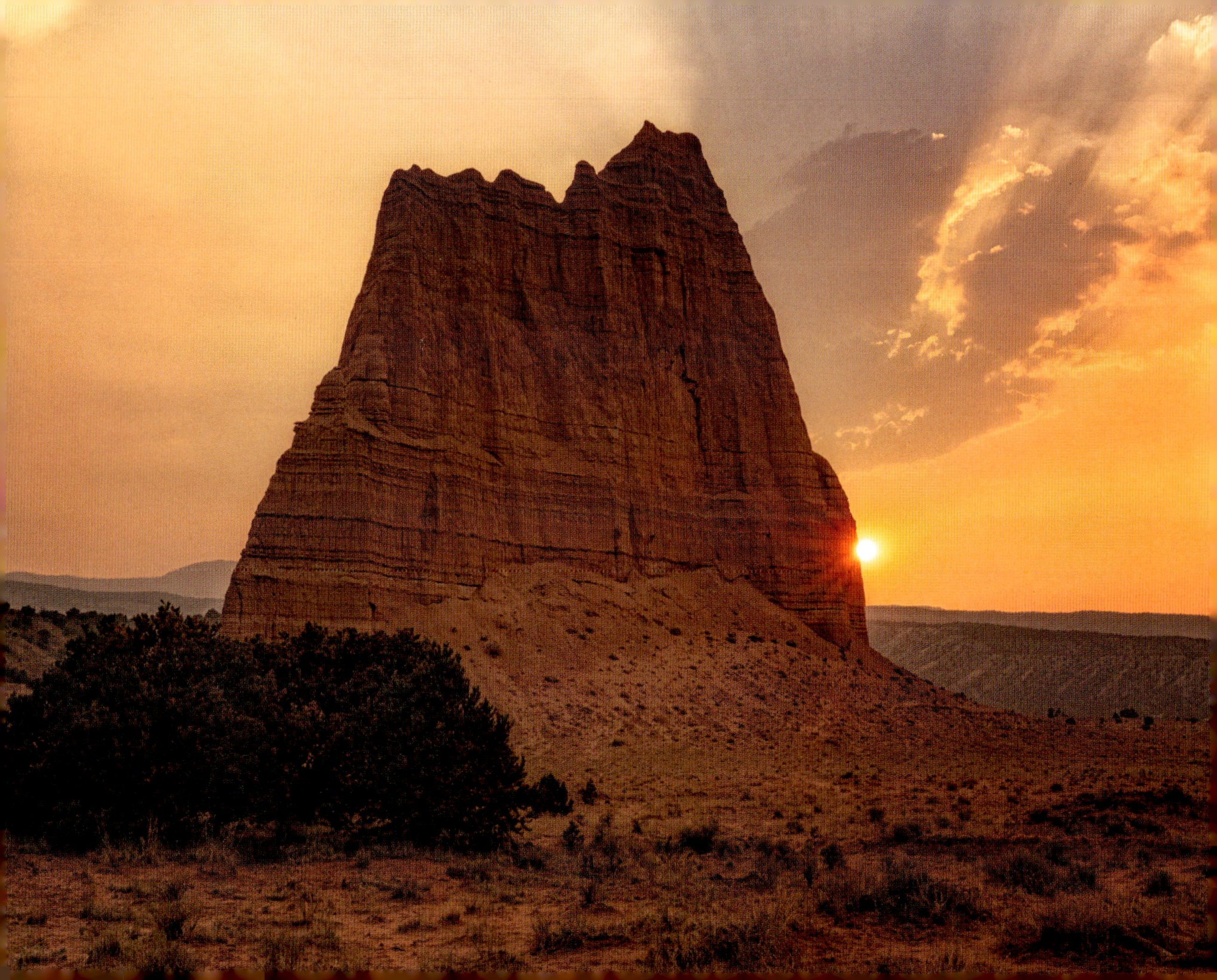

*Cathedral Valley, Capitol Reef National Park, Utah*

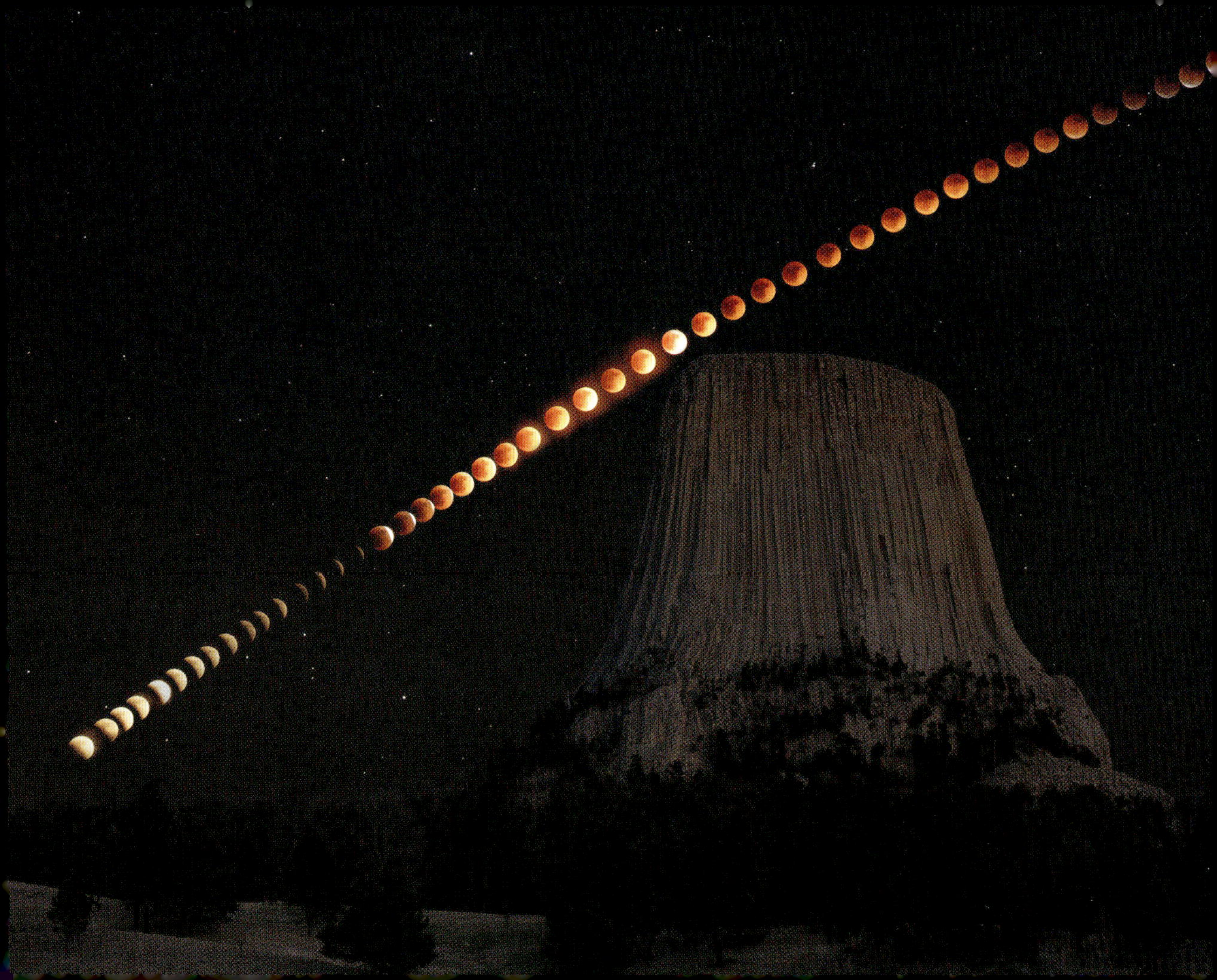

For me, photography is a Zen pursuit, freeing the mind to engage in a heightened awareness of time, light, and space. My enjoyment of photography outings increased as I became less overwhelmed with choosing camera settings and more concerned with composition and mood. Eventually, I realized that if I were more intentional with my preplanning, I would be freer to focus on the task at hand.

After months of planning, I arrived at Devils Tower National Monument about twelve hours before the first lunar eclipse of 2022, giving me the chance to hike around the base of the monument and scout out locations, but most importantly, to feel the sunshine on my face, smell the ponderosa pine, and hear the birdsong mixing with the murmur of the gentle breeze. I set up my camera about two hours before moonrise and waited. Six hours later, it was all over, yet time never felt both so fast and so irrelevant.

*Devils Tower National Monument, Wyoming*

Despite the careful planning that typically goes into a photographer's work, sometimes it just pays to be in the right place at the right time. That was certainly the case one early October evening when I found myself driving from Antonito, Colorado, to Santa Fe, New Mexico, on Highway 285, along the boundary of Carson National Forest. A thunderstorm swiftly moved in and, within minutes, had blocked out the night sky. After a few minutes, I began to see tiny strikes of lightning off in the distance. As I pulled off the road, a seam opened up above me and suddenly the Milky Way appeared over the tempest. A meteor decided to photobomb for added dramatic effect.

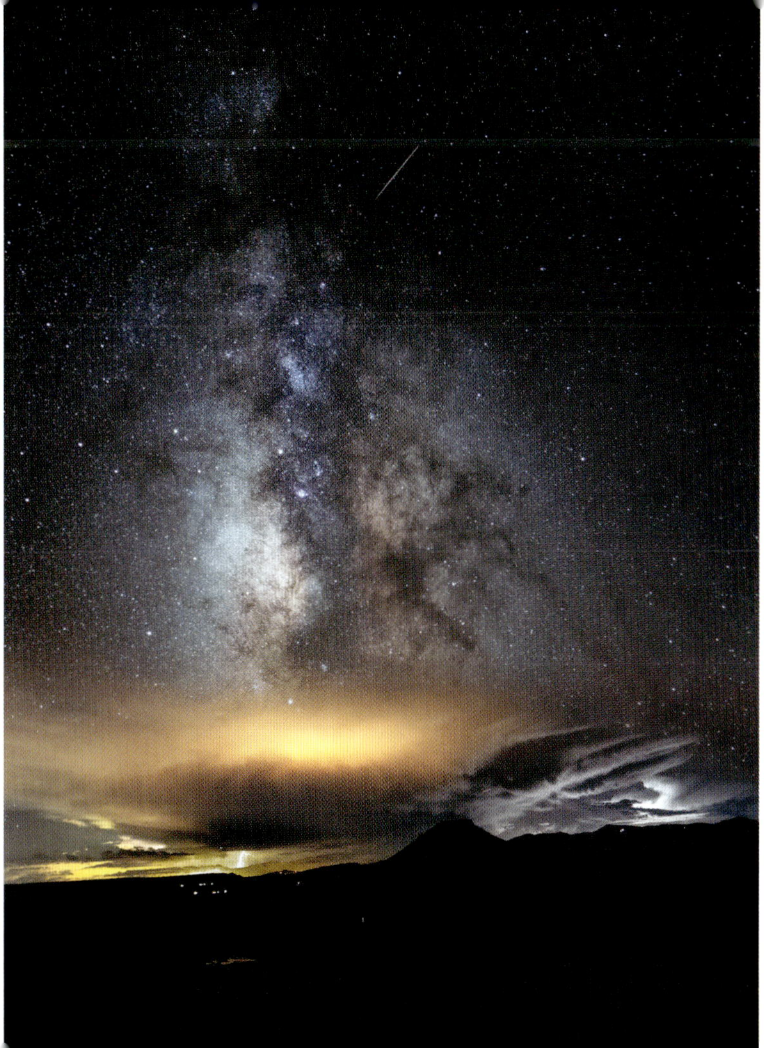

*Carson National Forest, New Mexico*

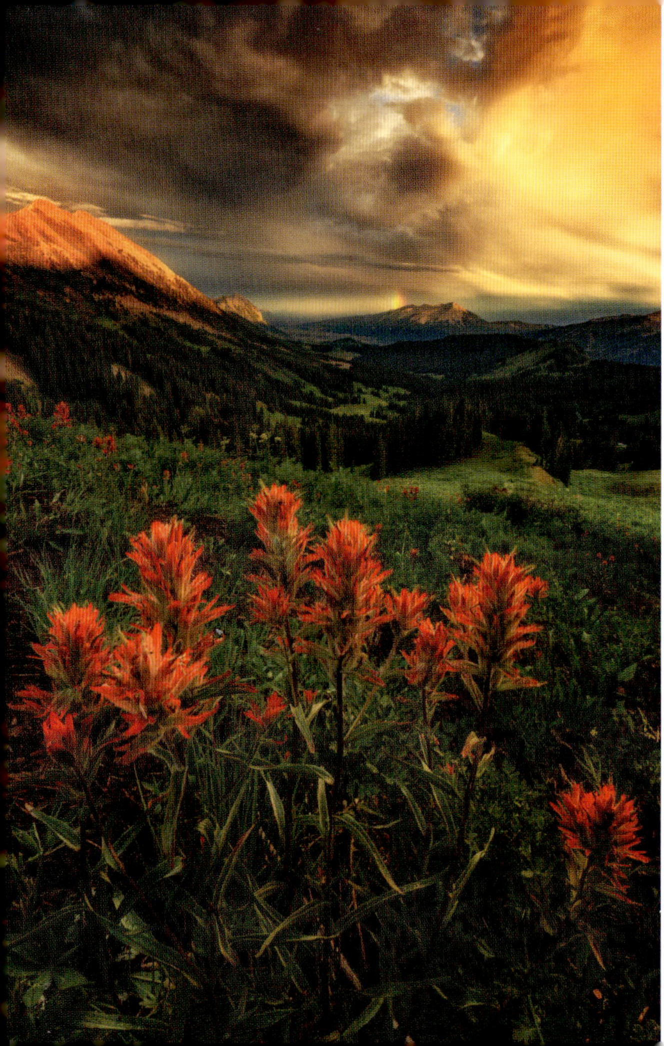
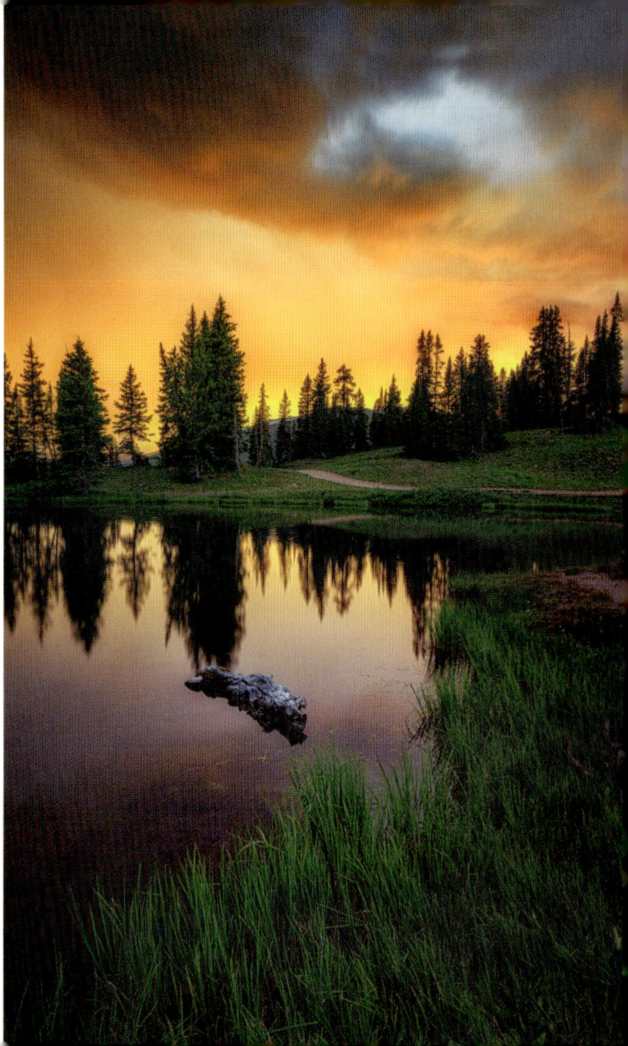

*Where the most beautiful wild flowers grow,*
*there man's spirit is fed and poets grow.*

—HENRY DAVID THOREAU, JOURNAL ENTRY,
JUNE 15, 1852

Left: *Washington Gulch, Crested Butte, Colorado*
Right: *Paradise Lake, Crested Butte, Colorado*

*Expose a child to a particular environment at his susceptible time and he will perceive in the shapes of that environment until he dies.*

—WALLACE STEGNER, *WOLF WILLOW*

As a boy, I spent many hours exploring my grandfather's farm in central Kentucky, whiling away golden summer days at the creek that ran through the lone patch of trees along its boundaries. I began every journey with the intention of locating its source but quickly lost interest in the destination as I stopped to see a crawdad, stomped through a shallow, or became mesmerized by the sun-dappled water lapping over the rocks.

Mornings stretched into middays and meandered into late afternoons. Eventually, I would trudge back home with tired legs and soggy shoes, pledging that next time—definitely, yes!—I would get serious and find the source of that stream.

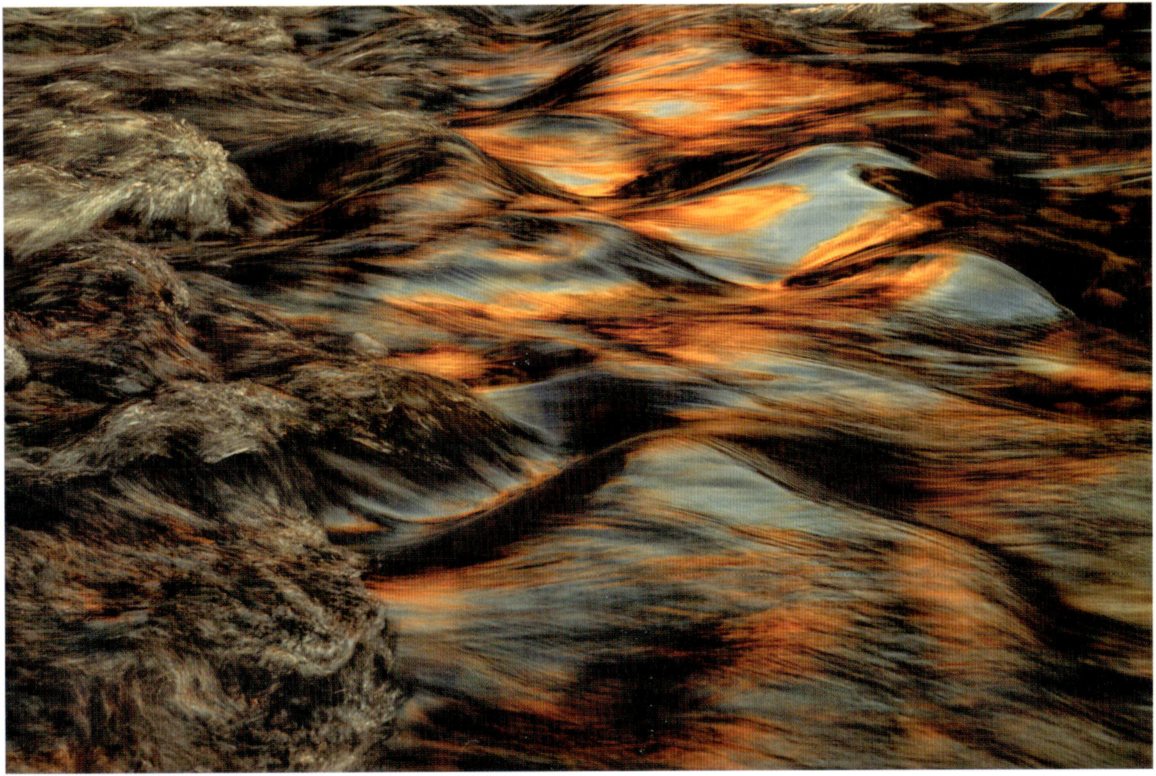

*Virgin River Narrows, Zion National Park, Utah*

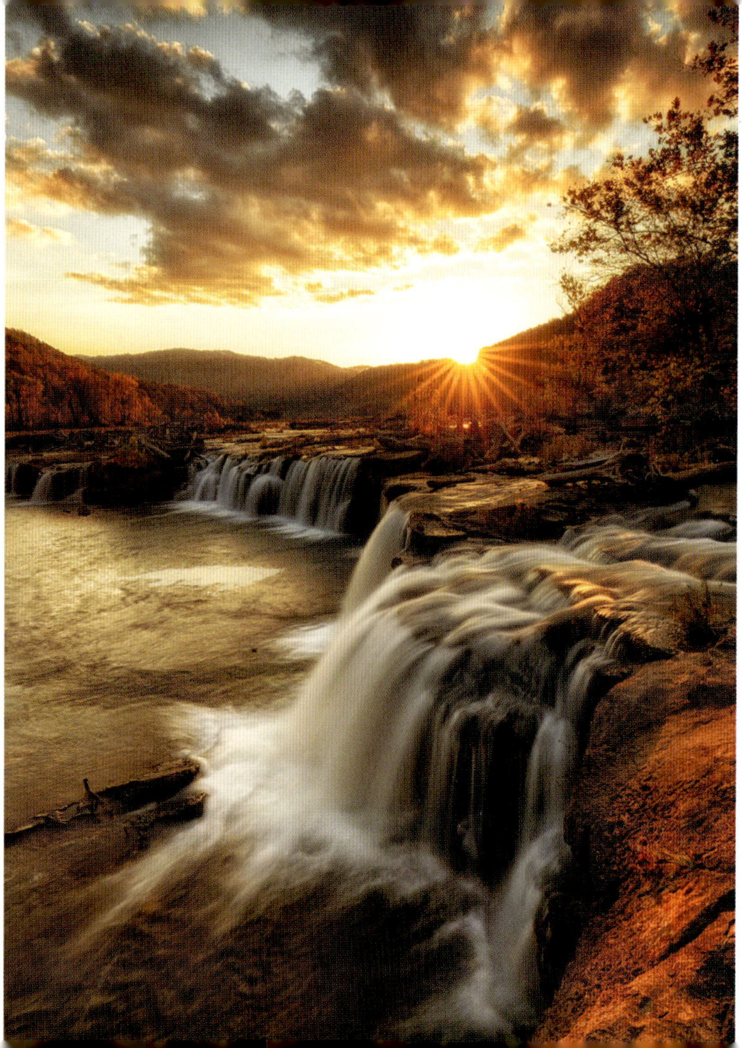

*Sandstone Falls, New River Gorge National Park, West Virginia*

Waterfalls have inherent visual interest, making them a natural subject for novice photographers learning the basics of the craft. Though many are located on well-trodden paths in state and national parks, many others require a divining rod and a star chart to find.

Sandstone Falls is a popular destination on the New River in West Virginia, but the first time I sought it out was during the El Niño winter of 2014, with six inches of snow on the road and a confused GPS sending me toward Irish Mountain Road, a euphemistically named gravel path three miles above my destination. As I left the edge of the world and began to descend into the blank space on the map, a tiny chihuahua marched out in front of me. I stopped. We locked eyes. "Go get help, boy," I pleaded. In response, he turned around and disappeared back down the driveway. Word of advice to all photography initiates: don't take advice from small dogs.

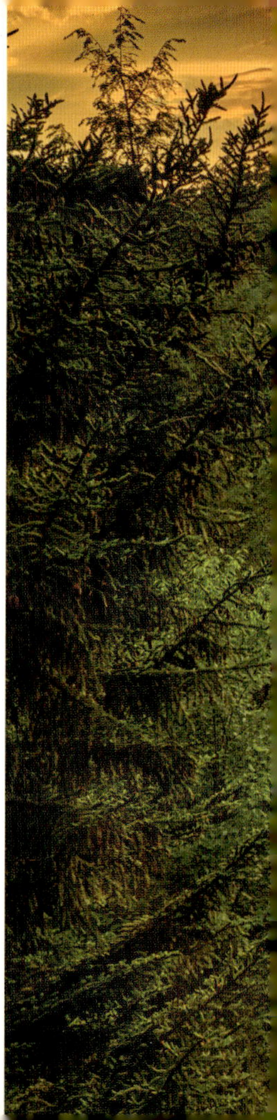

*Blackwater Falls State Park, West Virginia*

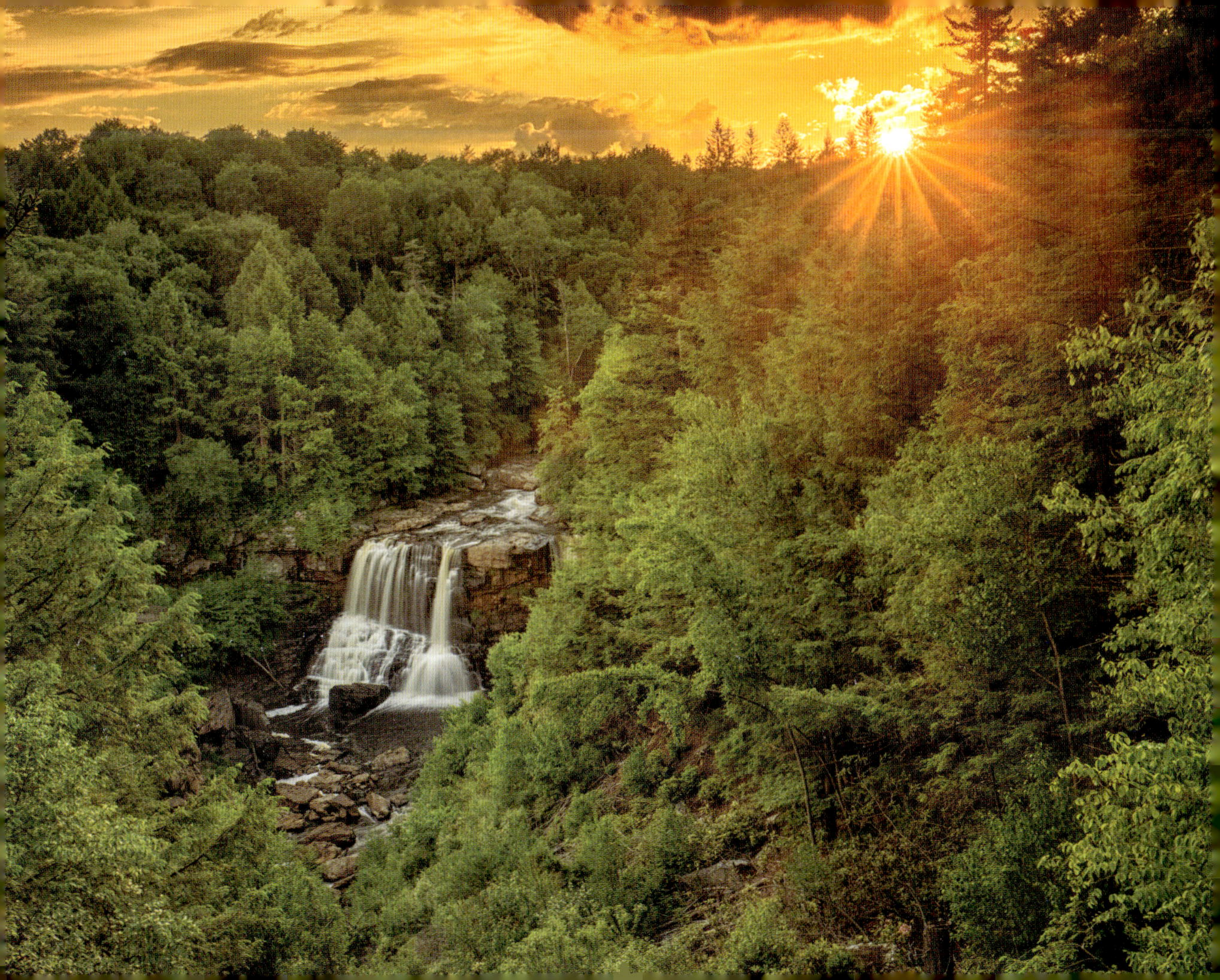

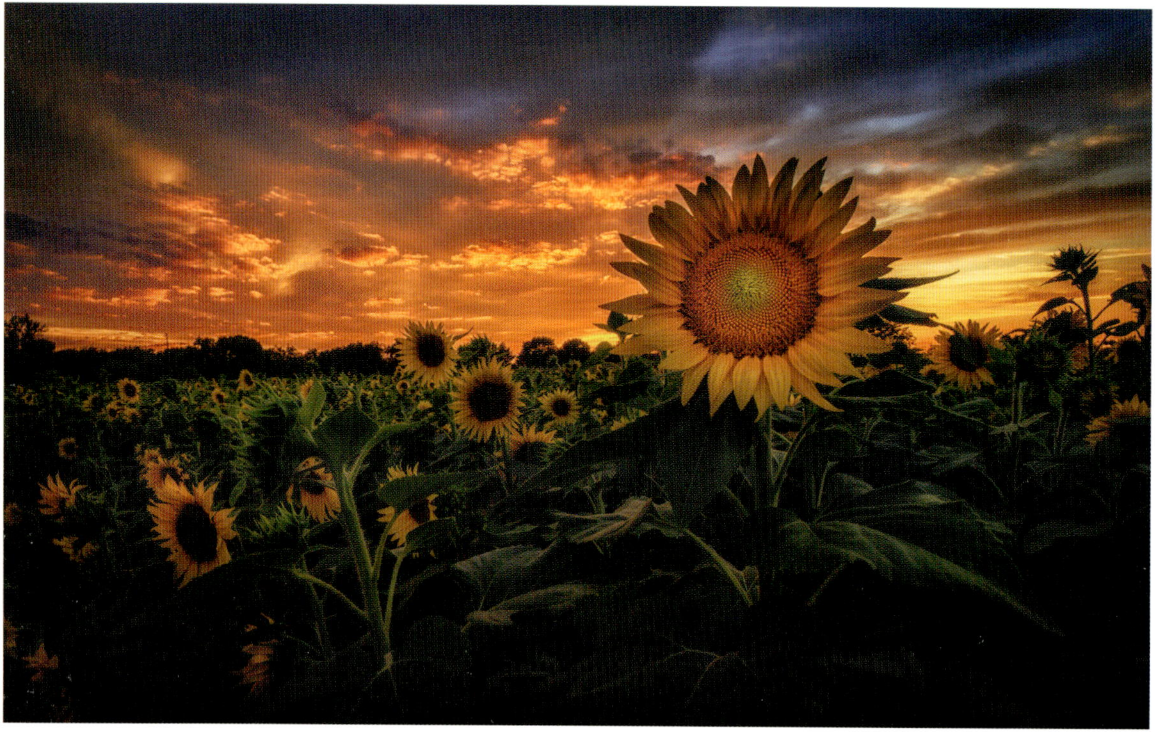

*A defiant sunflower rises at Gorman Heritage Farm, Evendale, Ohio.*

*Photography is a way of feeling, of touching, of loving. What you have caught on film is captured forever. . . . It remembers little things, long after you have forgotten everything.*

—AARON SISKIND

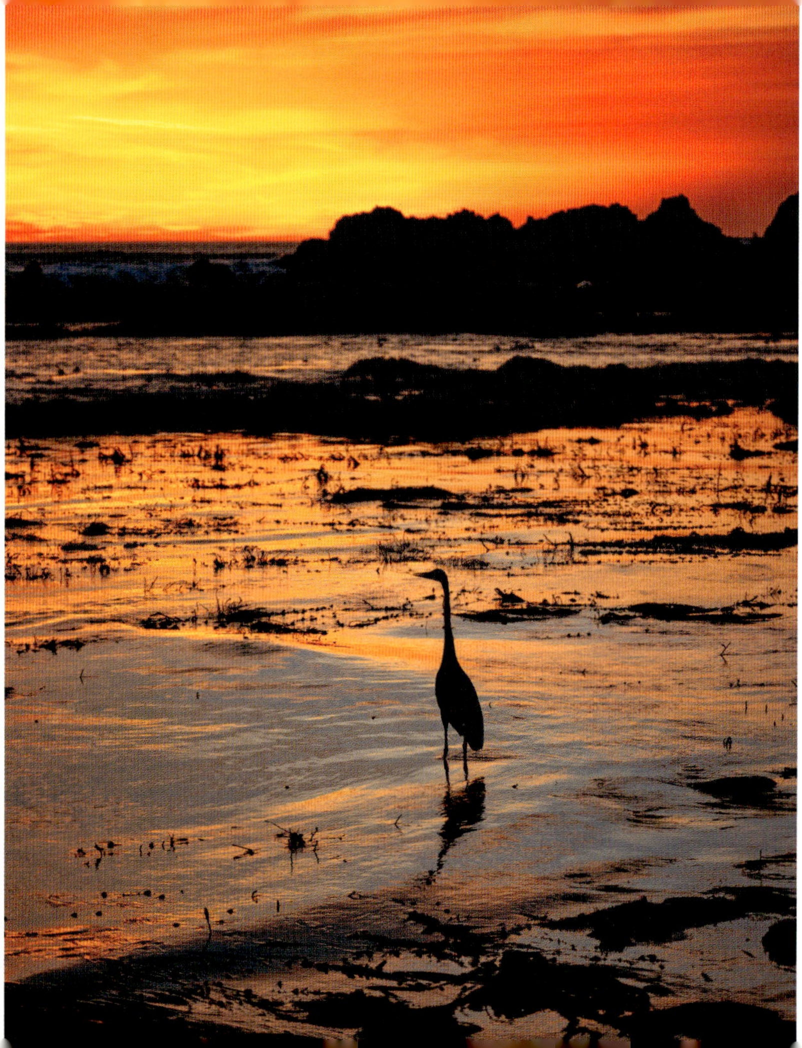

*Half Moon Bay, California*

*Whenever I have found myself stuck in the ways I relate to things, I return to nature. It is my principal teacher, and I try to open my whole being to what it has to say.*

—WYNN BULLOCK

A heron contemplates the end of day at Half Moon Bay. I had followed this little fellow all over the beach for over an hour, entranced by its economy of movement as it probed the tidal pools and shallows, and yet never seemed overly concerned about catching anything (unlike the fisherman who had been plying his trade long before I arrived and was constantly filling his basket). Suddenly, the sky began to blaze the most intense orange I had ever witnessed. To my surprise, the heron ended his pretense and joined in the admiration of nature's display.

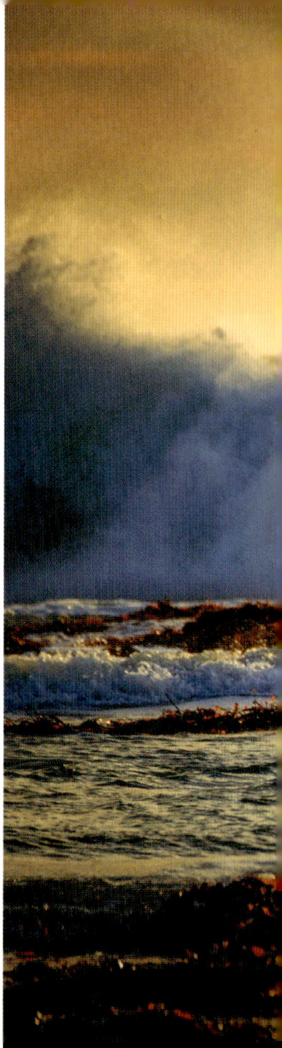

*Half Moon Bay, California*

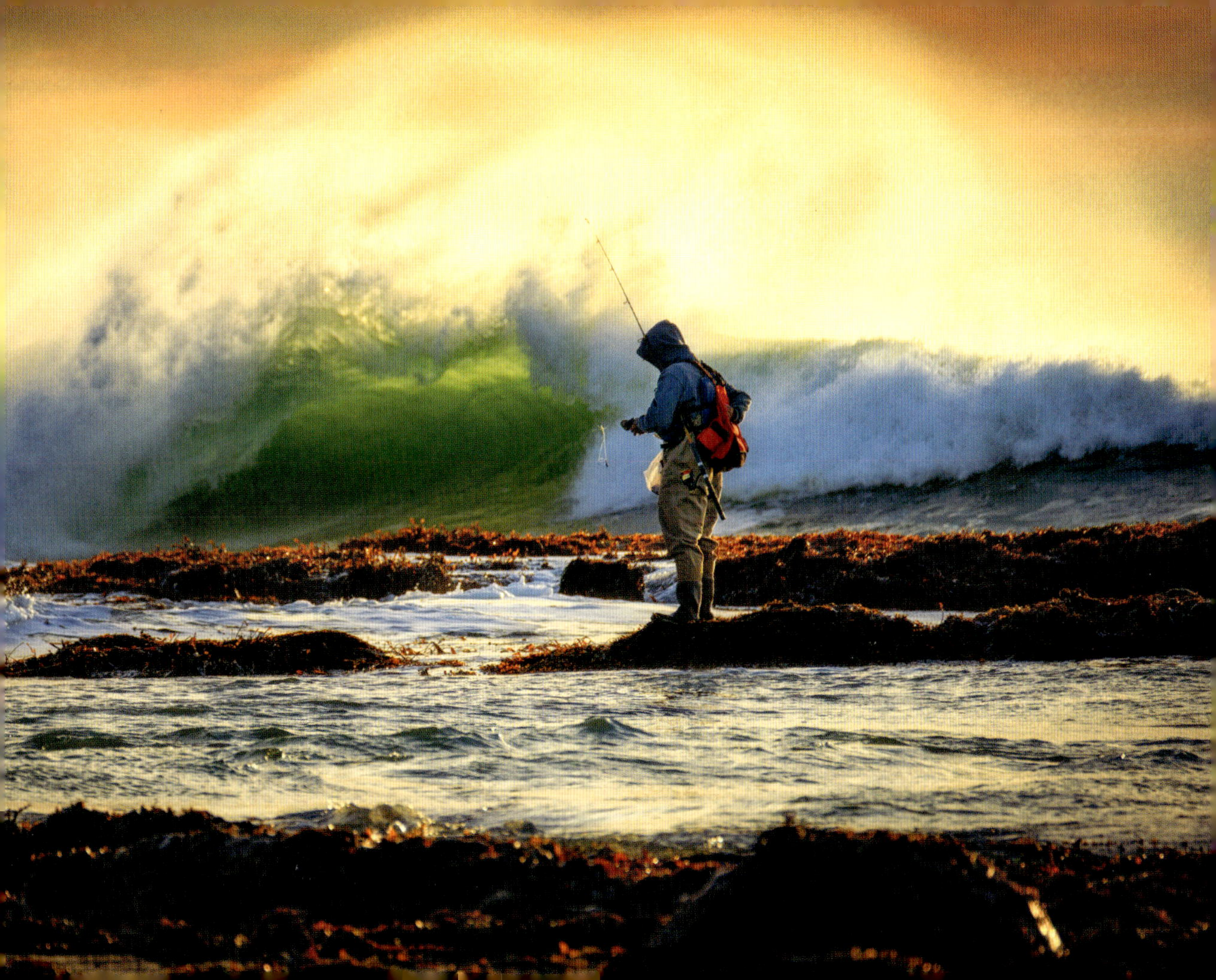

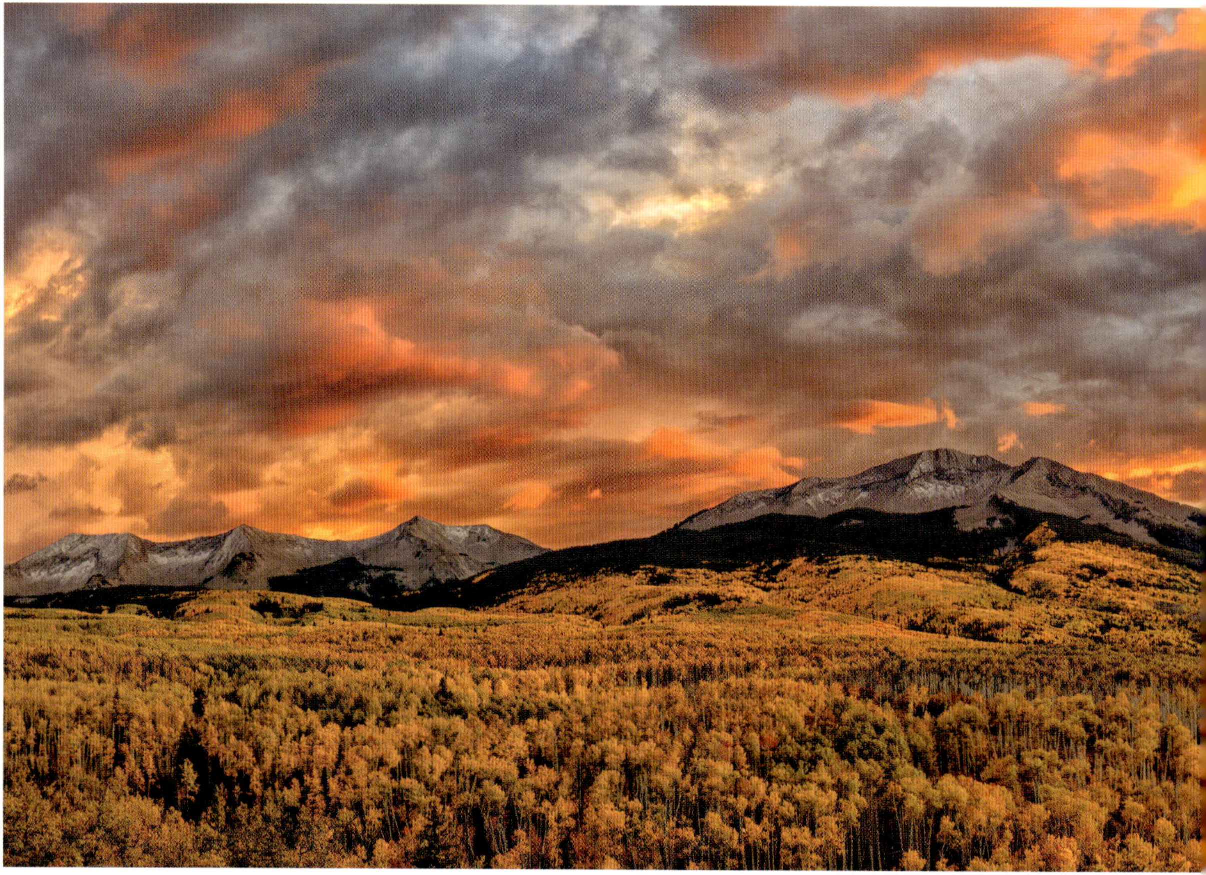

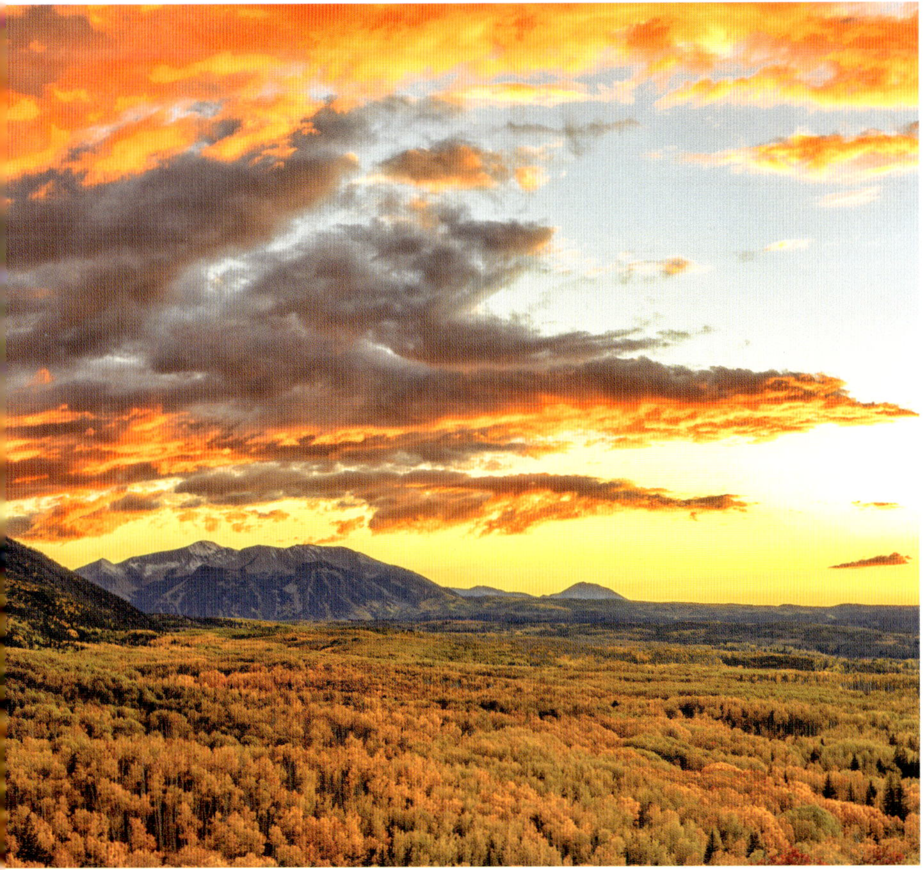

*Kebler Pass, Gunnison National Forest, Colorado*

"Well, that was epic," I mused out loud after the color had drained from the sky.

"Epic?! I should say!" the young man next to me huffed. "This was my third straight night here! It was about time!" We were the only two photographers along this beautiful bend at Kebler Pass in Gunnison National Forest.

When I returned to my car, my wife, who had been patiently waiting the whole time, looked over and smiled. "Well, what did you think?" she asked.

"Epic," I responded, echoing earlier sentiments.

"What was the other guy saying to you?"

"Oh, that he had been here three nights and hadn't had much success until tonight." I started the car. A long pause followed.

"Did you tell him that this was your only night here?" she asked.

"No," I replied. I turned to her, and we shared a knowing look.

"Smart move."

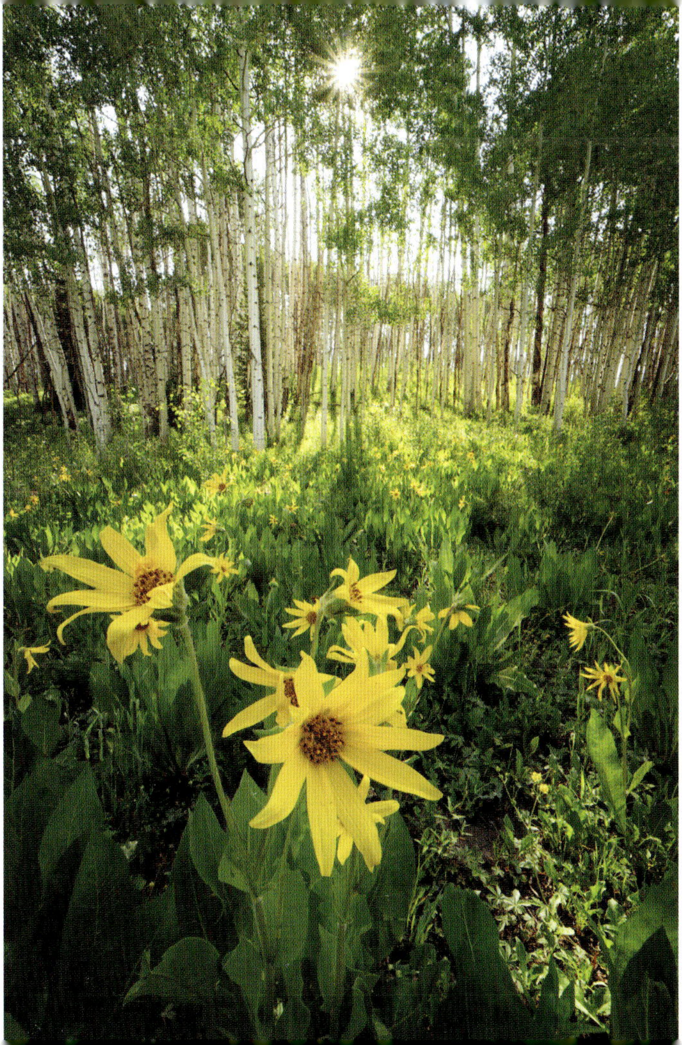

*Kebler Pass, Gunnison National Forest, Colorado*

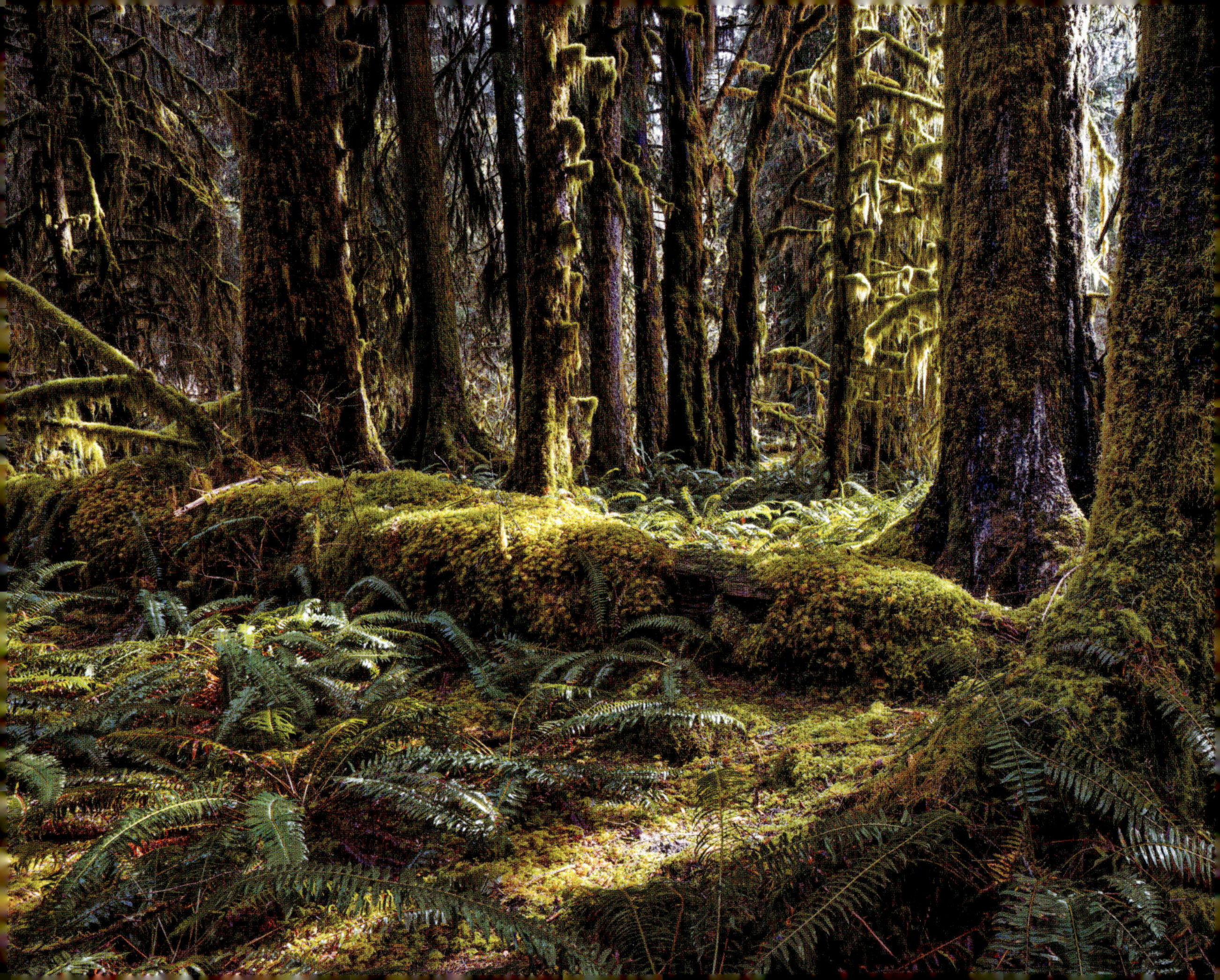

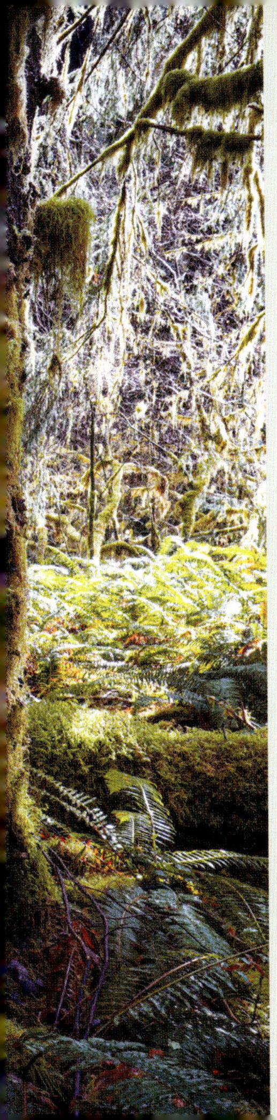

*Wilderness is not a luxury but a necessity of the human spirit, and as vital to our lives as water and good bread.*

—EDWARD ABBEY, *DESERT SOLITAIRE*

*Hoh Rain Forest, Olympic National Park, Washington*

In 2020, the Elkmont section of the Great Smoky Mountains National Park near Gatlinburg, Tennessee, was closed and the annual Synchronous Firefly Festival canceled due to the pandemic. The entrance road was still accessible by foot, so in early June I hiked in, warily stepping off to the side of the road to anticipate an imaginary stream of cars that normally would be zipping up and down this well-visited section of the park.

The only rush I encountered was the roaring Little River, mixed with the jubilant chirping of birds thankful for a respite from the hordes of tourists. These soothing sounds soon faded into the eerie quiet of an empty road and shuttered campground. For almost two hours, I was the lone human interloper, greeted only once by a couple riding their bikes back toward the entrance.

Still somewhat uncomprehending my situation, I set up along the trail and nervously began to wait. After a few minutes the unsettled feeling of isolation gave way to anticipation of this amazing yearly ritual.

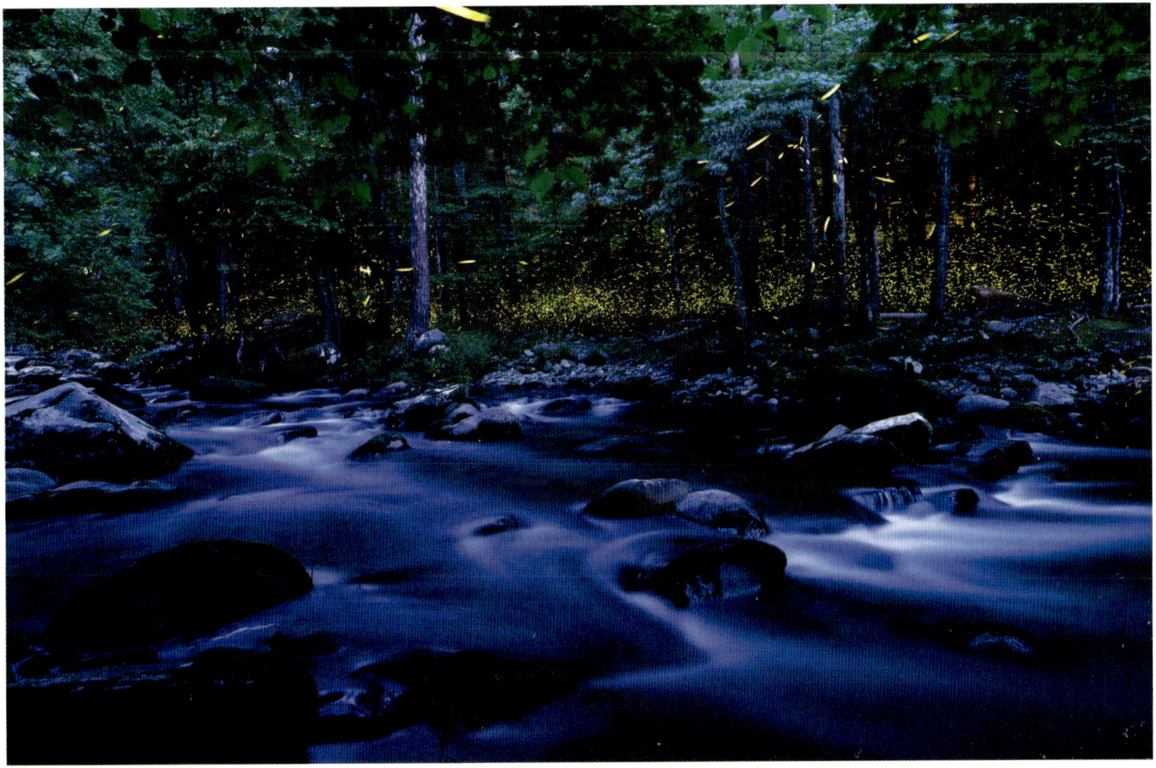

*Great Smoky Mountains National Park, Tennessee*

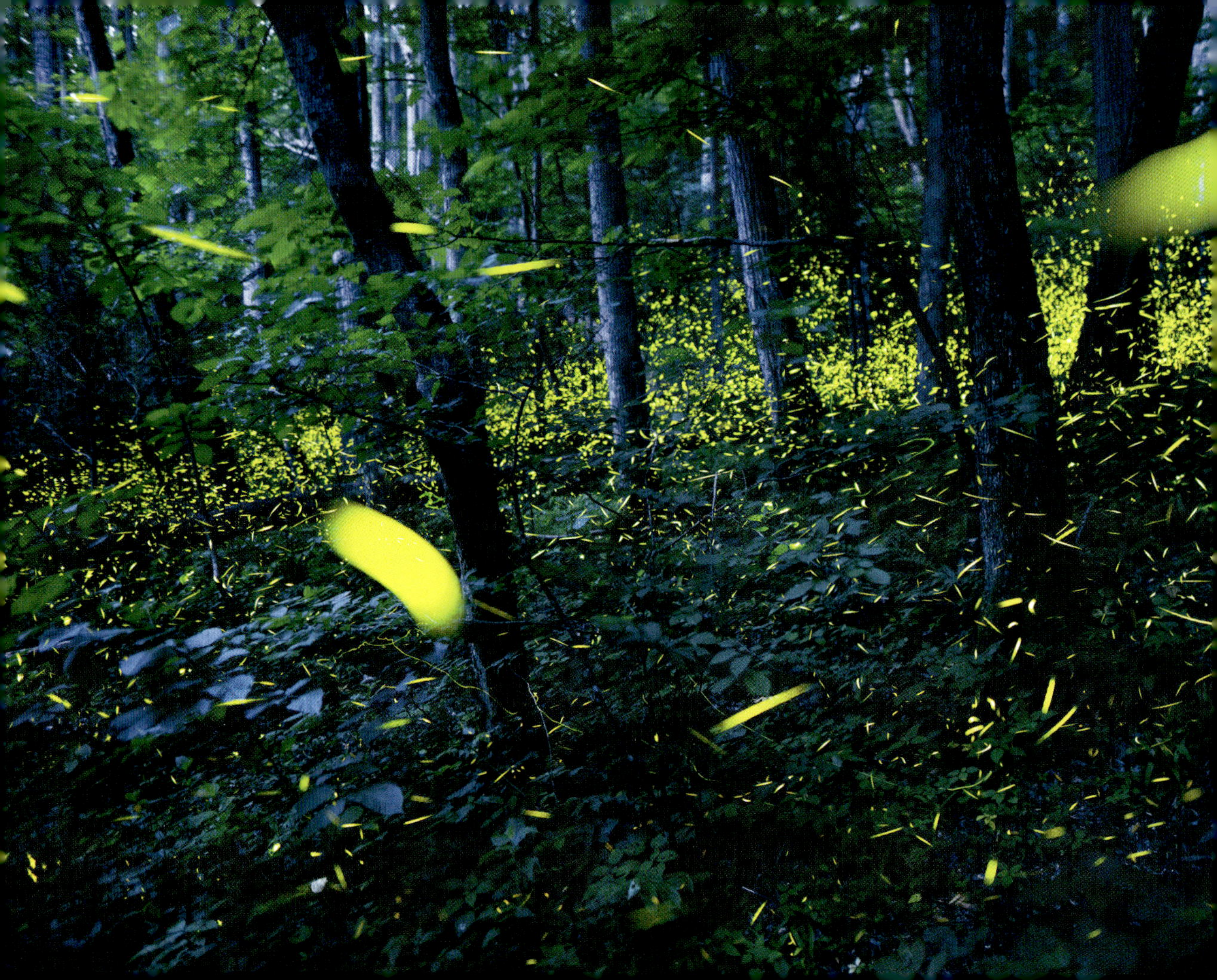

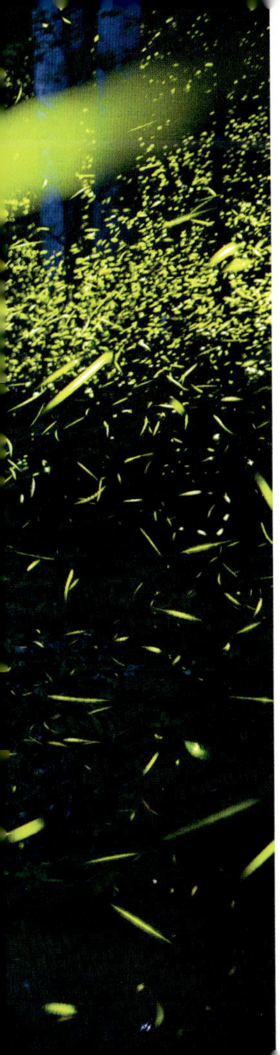

Little by little, they begin—silent sparks tapping out a fiery Morse code, increasing in intensity as daylight fades and the deep emerald of the forest recedes into darkness.

As night descends, the synchronous fireflies—*Photinus carolinus*—fill the woods with the deafening roar of illuminated silence.

Finally, they fully merge into a single, glowing pulse, the incandescent heart-light of the Smokies.

*Great Smoky Mountains National Park, Tennessee*

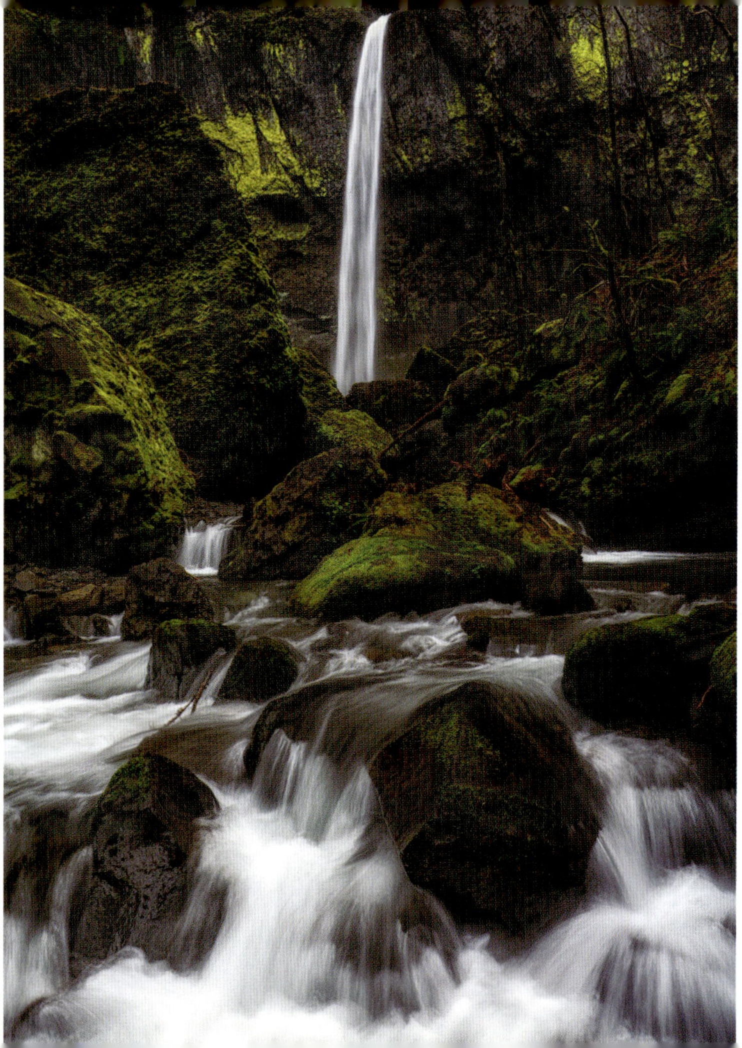

*Elowah Falls, Oregon*

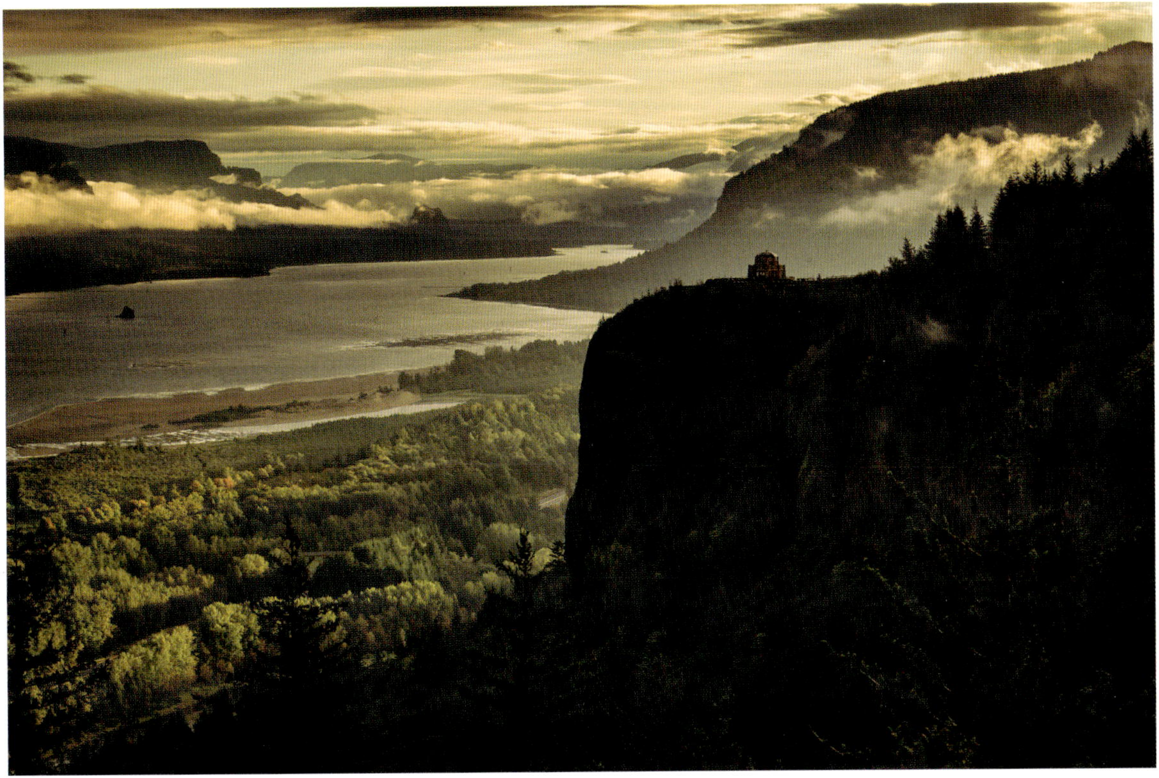

*A view of the Vista House at Crown Point, located along the Historic Columbia River Highway in Multnomah County, Oregon.*

*Nature's first green is gold,*
*Her hardest hue to hold.*
*Her early leaf's a flower;*
*But only so an hour.*
*Then leaf subsides to leaf.*
*So Eden sank to grief,*
*So dawn goes down to day.*
*Nothing gold can stay.*

—ROBERT FROST, "NOTHING GOLD CAN STAY"

Left: *Unnamed road, Vermont*
Right: *Owl Creek Pass, Colorado*

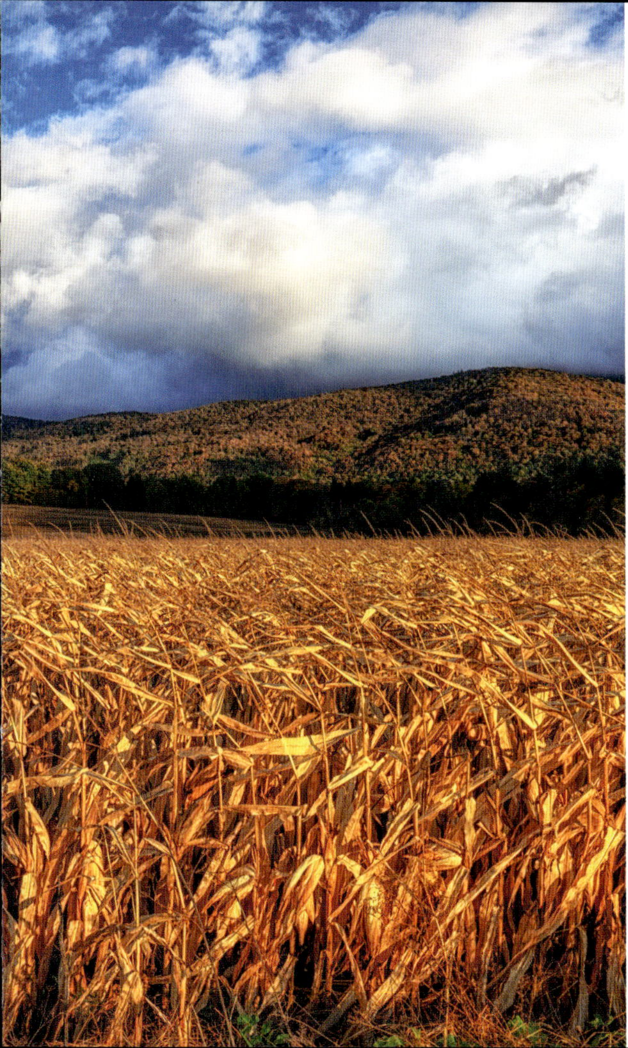
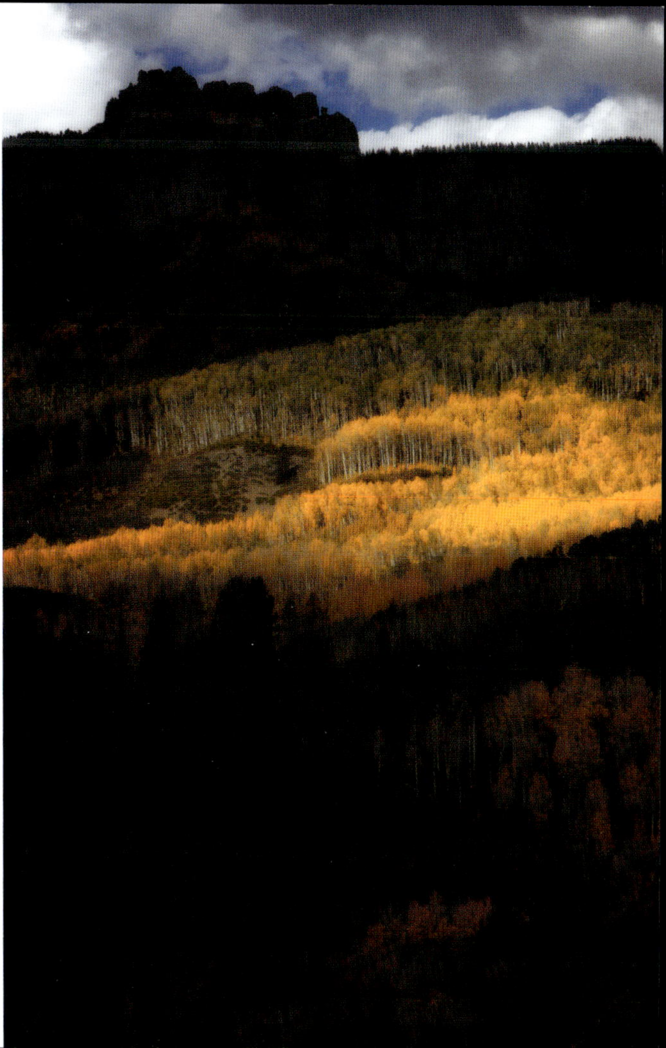

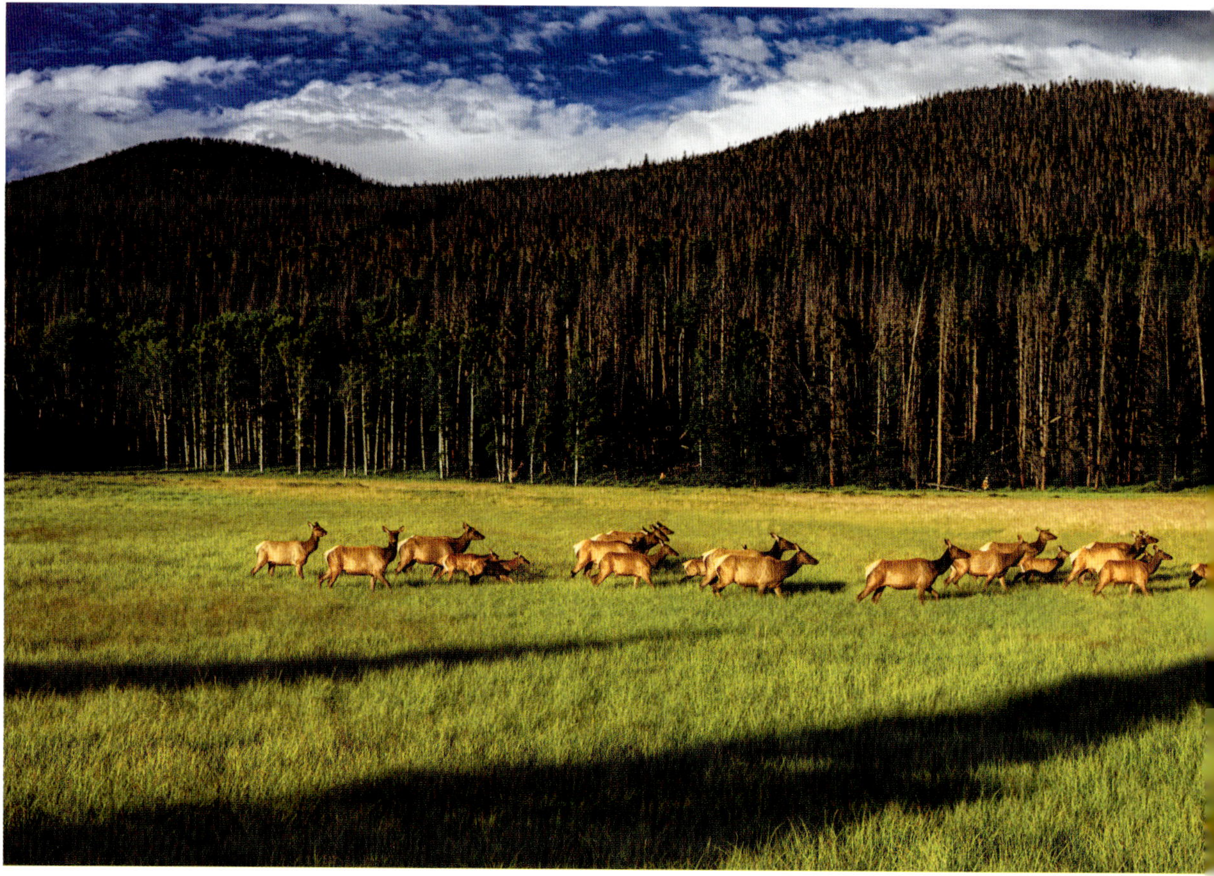

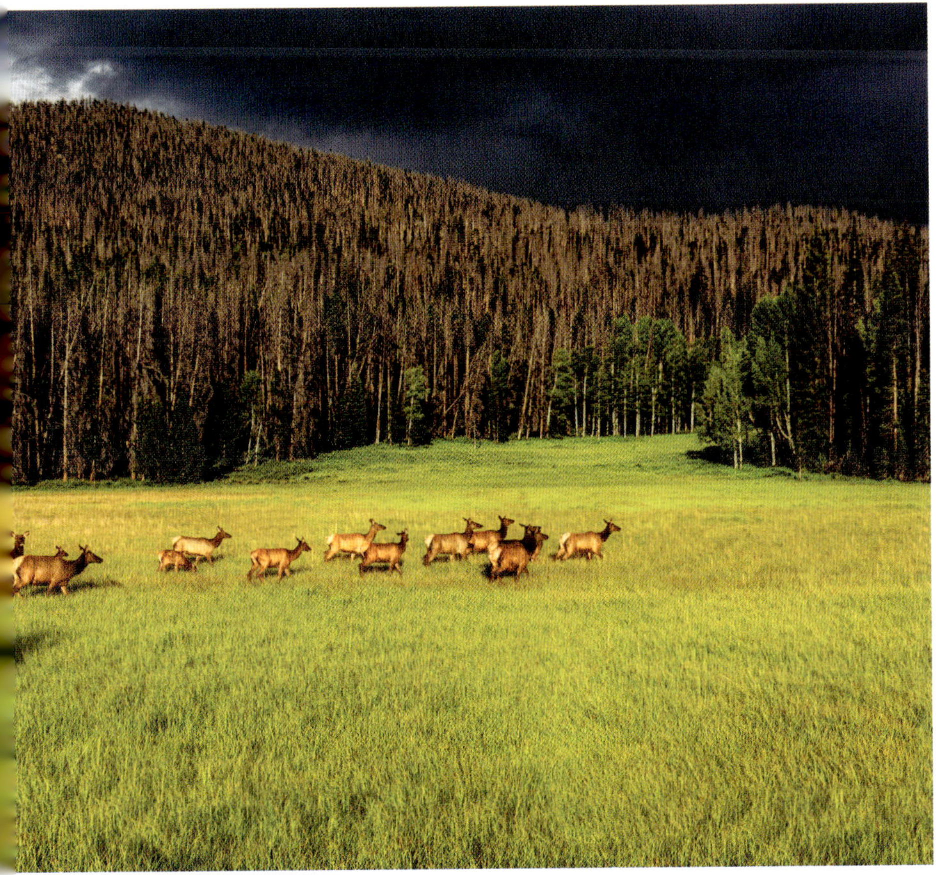

*In late summer, a month or so before the famed elk rut, a herd begins its afternoon rush-hour return to the lower meadows near the Grand Lake entrance to Rocky Mountain National Park, Colorado.*

*Peanut Lake, Crested Butte, Colorado*

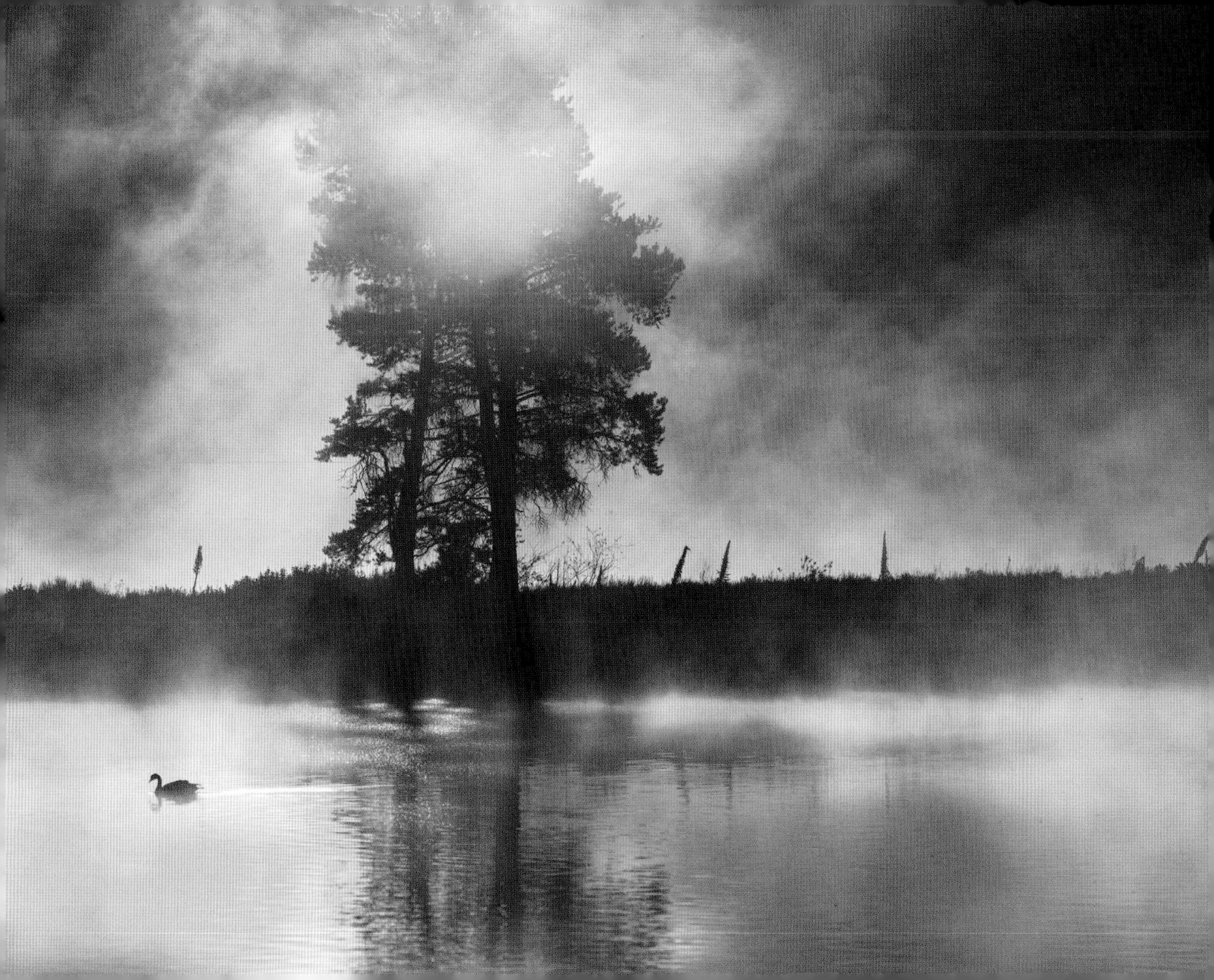

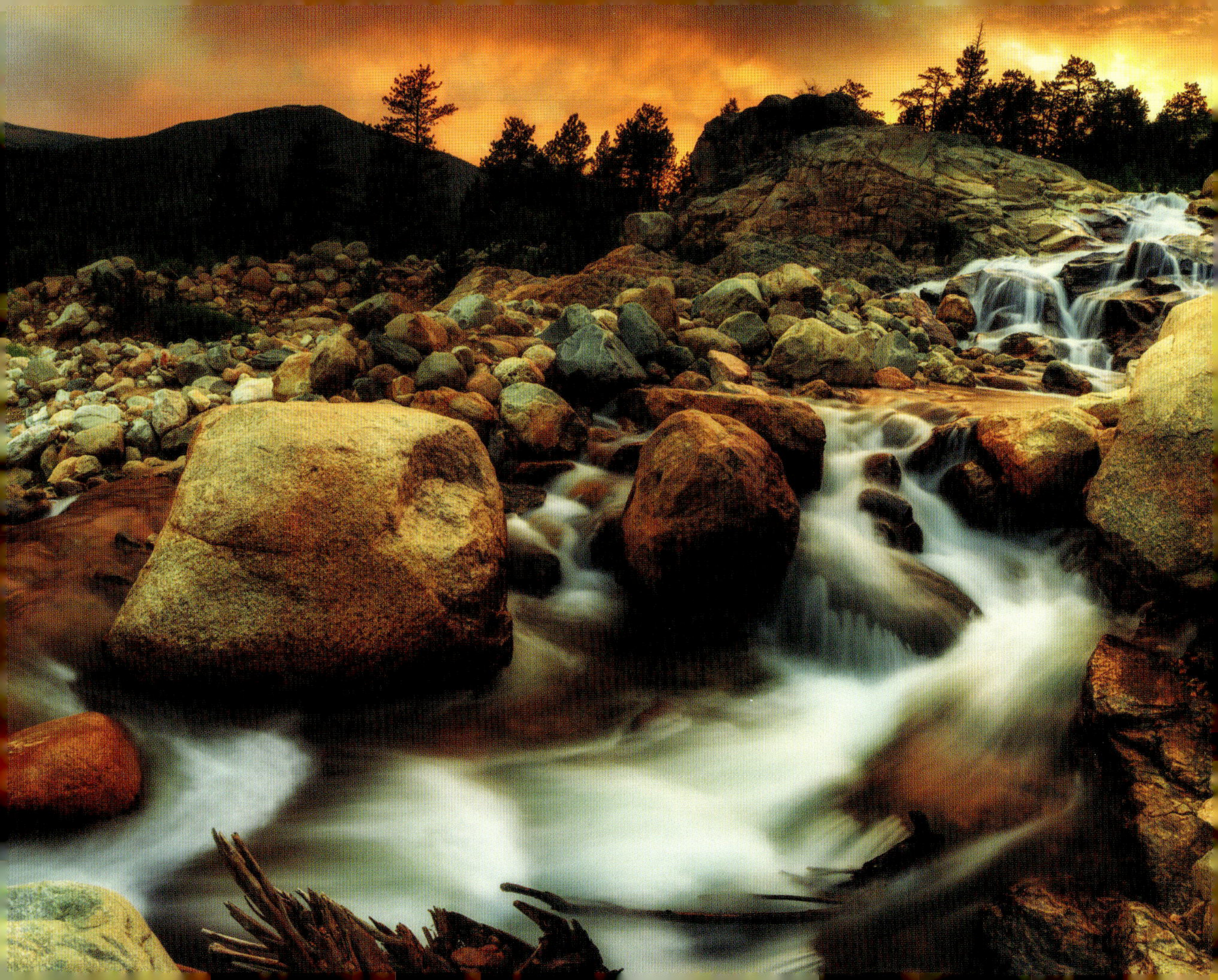

*I gave my heart to the mountains the minute I stood beside this river with its spray in my face and watched it thunder into foam, smooth to green glass over sunken rocks, shatter to foam again. I was fascinated by how it sped by and yet was always there; its roar shook both the earth and me.*

—WALLACE STEGNER, *THE SOUND OF MOUNTAIN WATER*

*Alluvial Fan, Rocky Mountain National Park, Colorado*

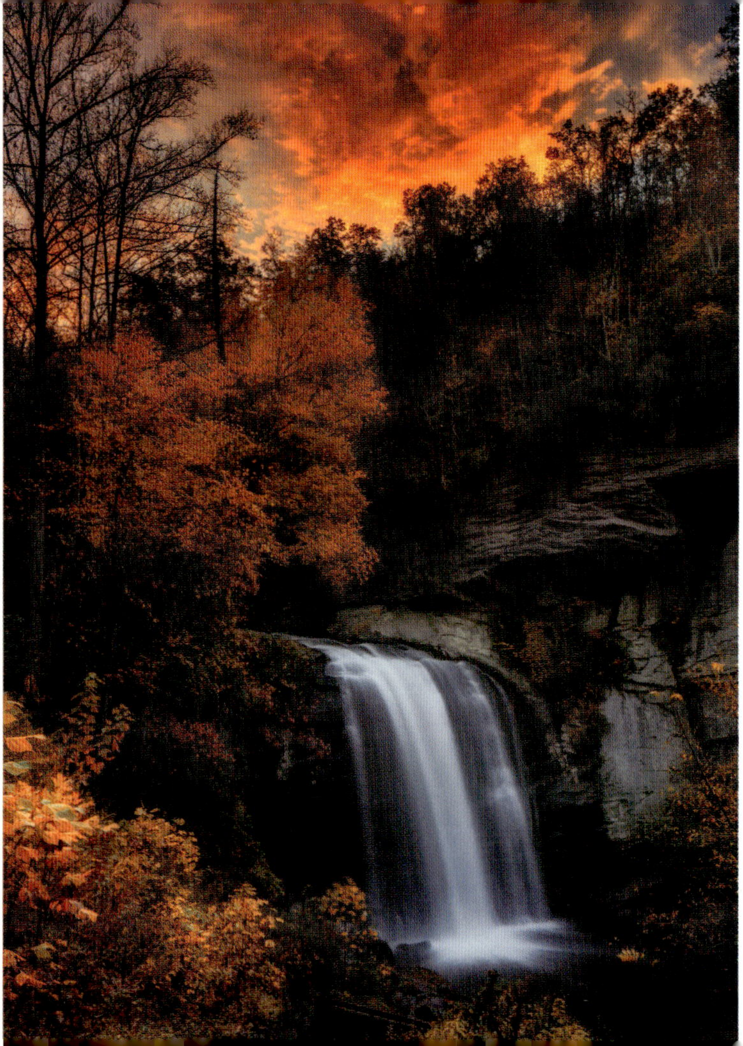

*Looking Glass Falls,*
*Pisgah National Forest,*
*North Carolina*

As a novice photographer you are overwhelmed with decisions and distractions—camera settings, malfunctioning gear, uncooperative weather. An earlier visit to Looking Glass Falls proved tremendously disappointing as I struggled with these fundamental challenges to my conscious mind. I vowed to keep learning, breaking down each element until I could develop a sense of automaticity and free my subconscious mind to take over. Six years and dozens of waterfalls and streams later I returned, more assured, more prepared.

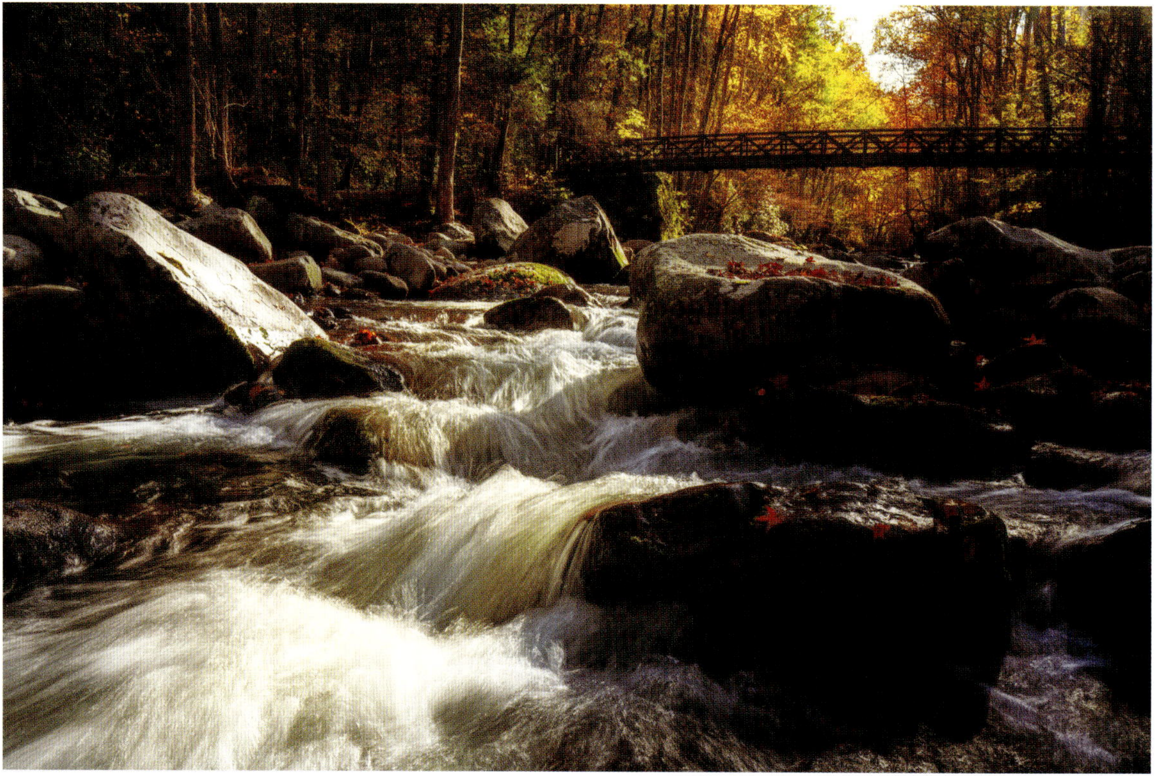

Left: *Big Creek, Great Smoky Mountains National Park, North Carolina*
Right: *Watkins Glen State Park, New York*

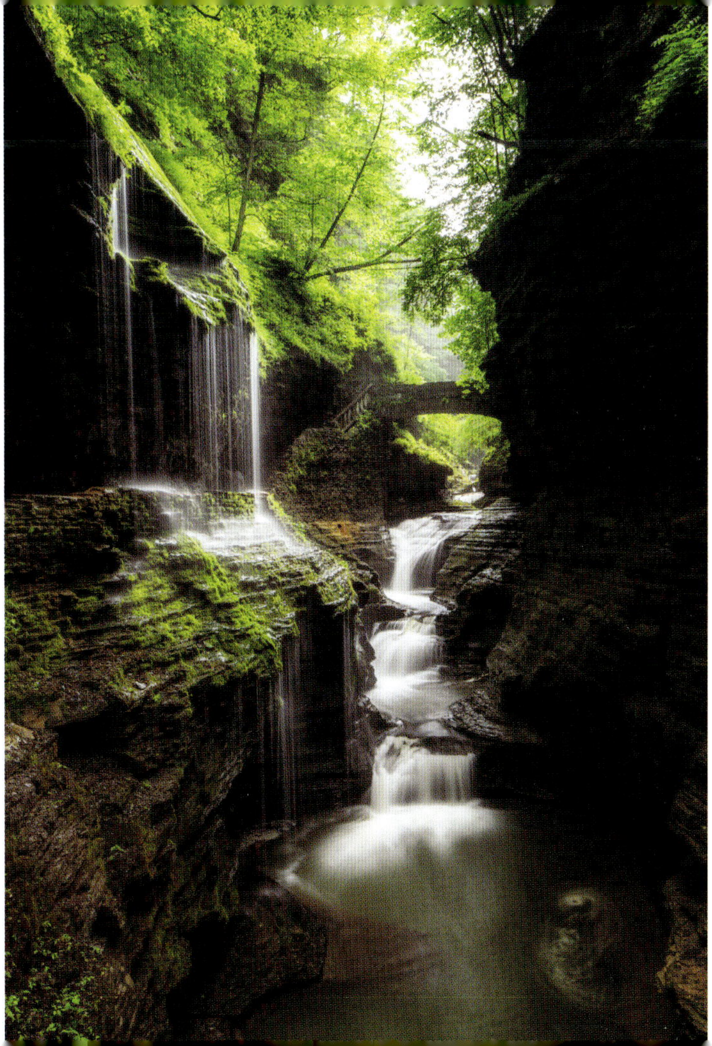

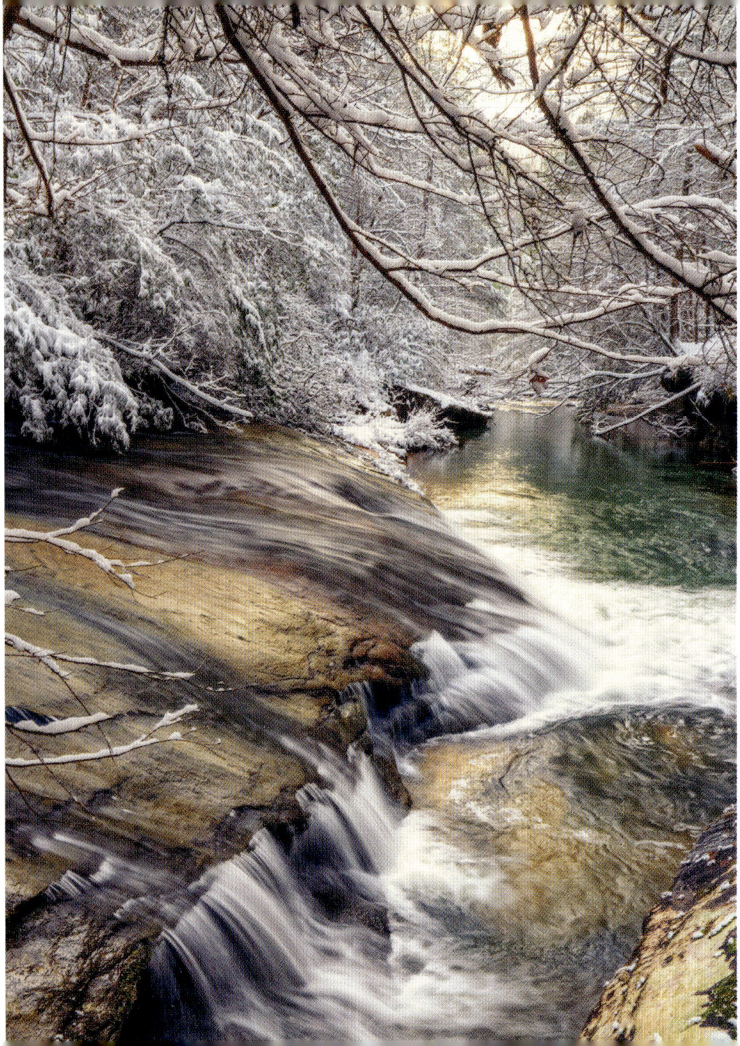

*A rare snowy day in early March at Eagle Creek, Cumberland Falls State Resort Park, Kentucky.*

*But if there is a state where the soul can find a resting-place secure enough to establish itself and concentrate its entire being there, with no need to remember the past or reach into the future, . . . we can call ourselves happy.*

—JEAN-JACQUES ROUSSEAU, *MEDITATIONS OF A SOLITARY WALKER*

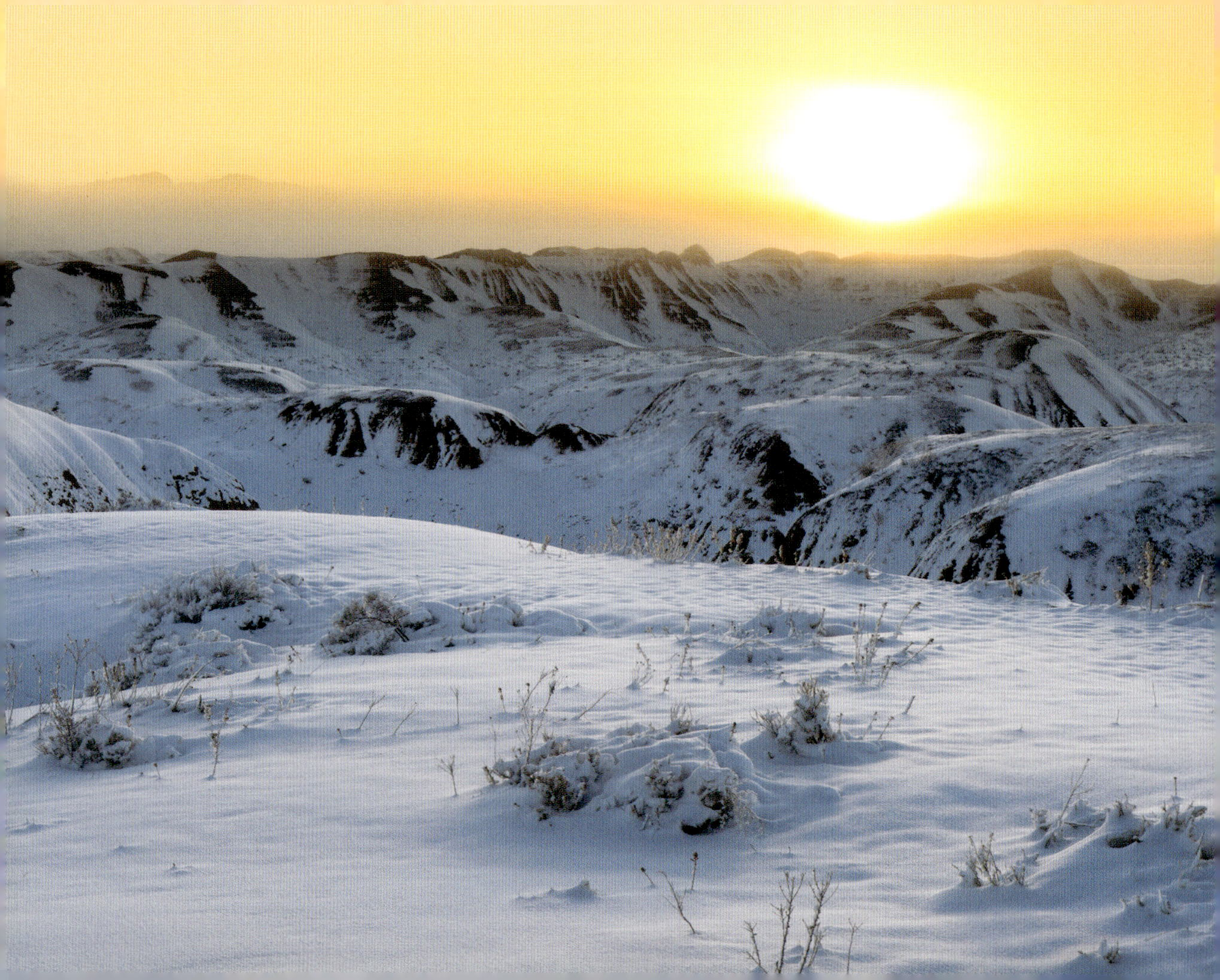

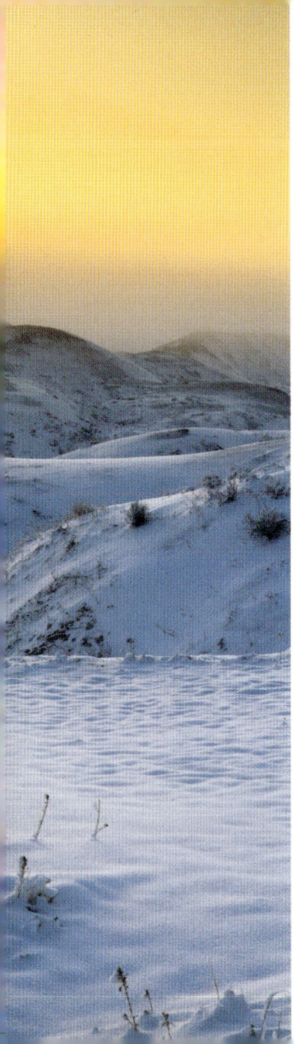

I entered Badlands National Park in South Dakota in the early morning during an intense prairie blizzard reminiscent of something out of Laura Ingalls Wilder. I managed to capture some pictures of bighorn sheep and buffalo huddling against the storm, but as the snow intensified, I decided to pack it in and head back to the hotel. The next morning, the storm had cleared out. Ridges along the north entrance that were otherwise unremarkable were now resplendent in white and glowing in the misty orange sunrise.

*Badlands National Park, South Dakota*

*And as the eye is the best composer, so light is the first of painters. There is no object so foul that intense light will not make beautiful.*

—RALPH WALDO EMERSON, *NATURE*

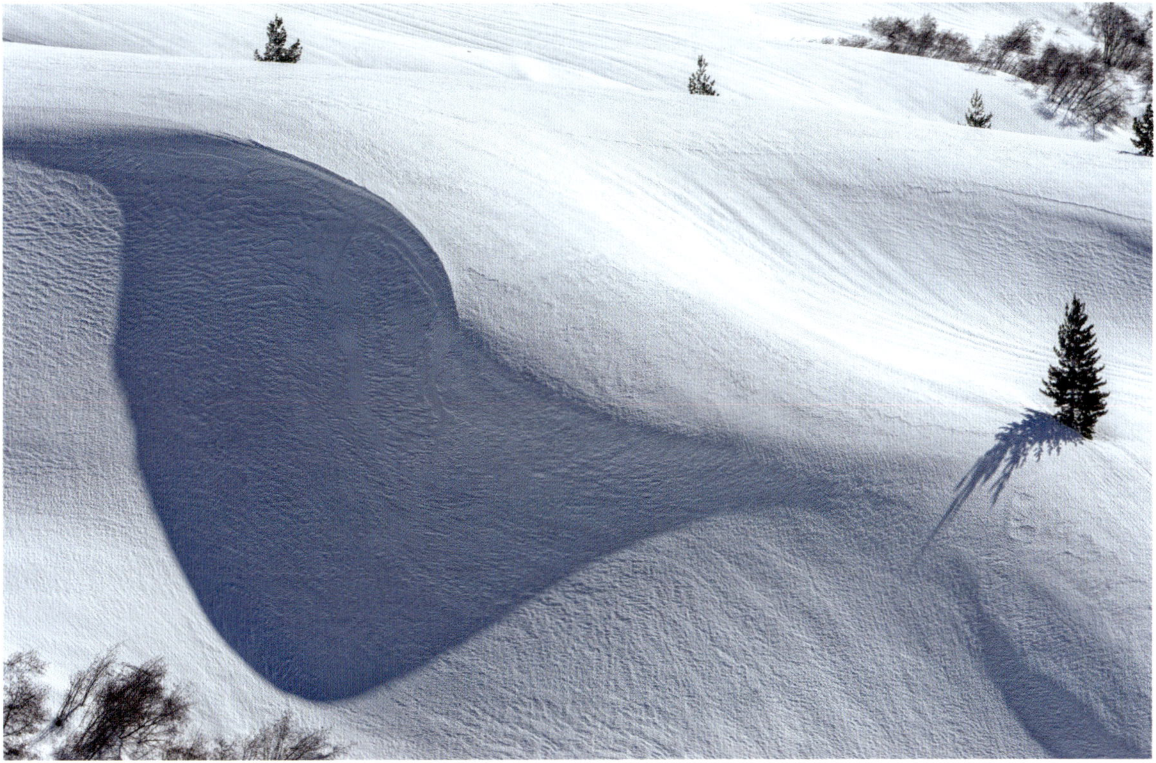

*Lassen Volcanic National Park, California*

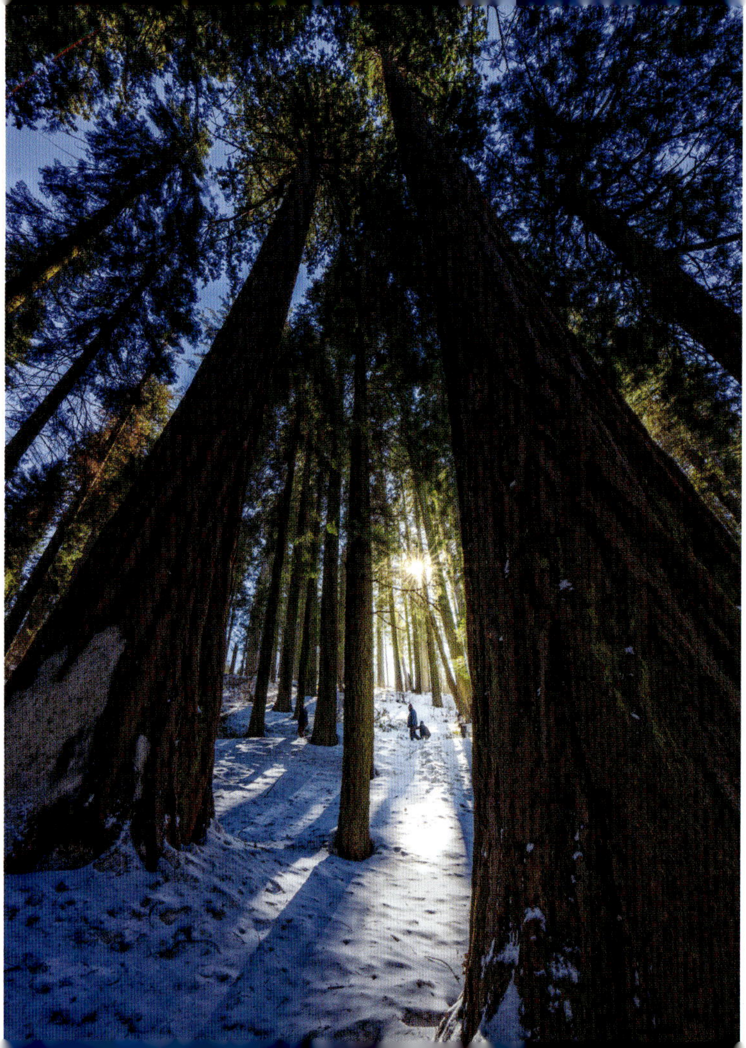

*Sequoia National Park, California*

*[It] is all too clear that every surviving oak is the product either of rabbit negligence or of rabbit scarcity.*

—ALDO LEOPOLD, *A SAND COUNTY ALMANAC*

In Sequoia National Park, the presence of the Sequoioideae demands reflection and contemplation. Unlike Half Dome in Yosemite—a geological monument forged long ago in some dim, distant past—the giant trees present an interesting paradox. At first you feel they are wrenched from the earth, their immense trunks strong and unyielding as visitors dart around them like busy ants. As you begin to crane your neck up, following the long, rhythmic lines of the bark skyward, you notice something interesting. Instead of standing like immovable sentinels, the tops sway in the breeze like the fingers of a giant hand slowly shaking off the effects of sleep. You rest your eyes at your feet to regain your senses, and that's when you see it: a sapling, drooping in the heavy wet snow. Later, you notice giant stumps scattered throughout the rolling forest. Birth and death. In the distance you hear the scampering of tiny feet against the frozen ground—a woodland creature, eager to reprise its role of nature's midwife.

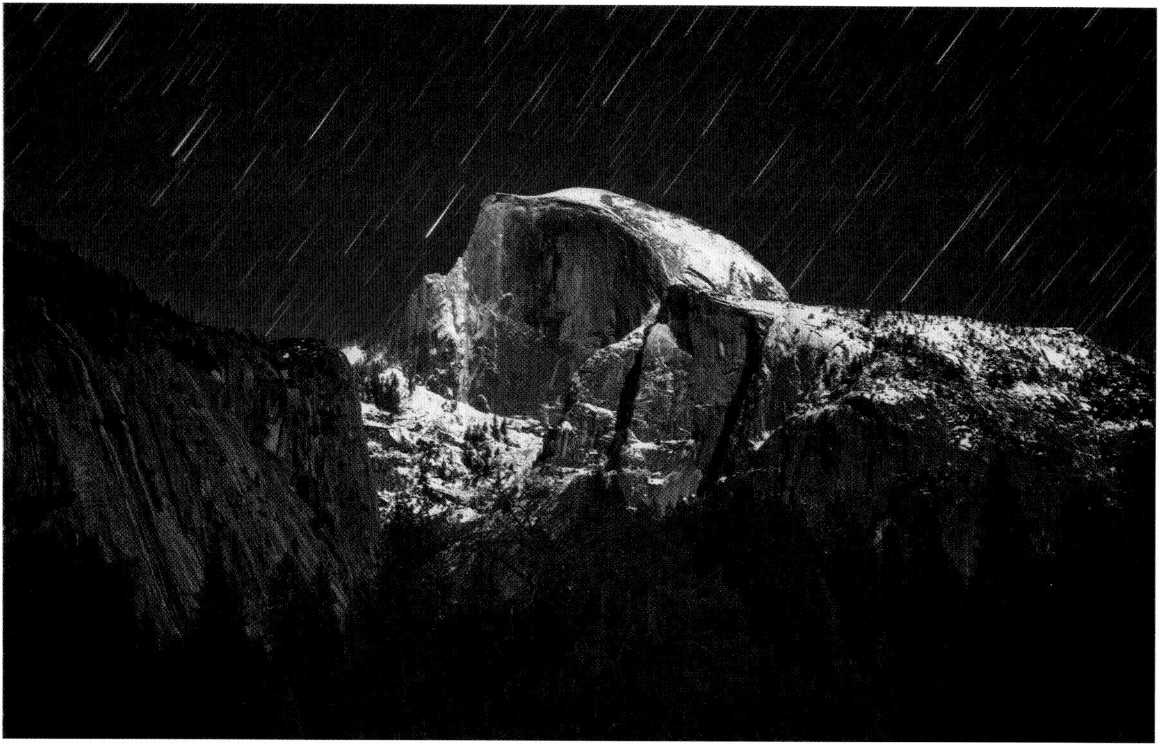

*Composite photo taken at Yosemite National Park, California, on a clear New Year's night, with a full moon illuminating the face of Half Dome.*

*Oh, these vast, calm, measureless mountain days, inciting at once to work and rest! Days in whose light everything seems equally divine, opening a thousand windows to show us God.*

—JOHN MUIR, *MY FIRST SUMMER IN THE SIERRA*

I had spent the entire night shooting the lunar eclipse and, after catching a couple hours of sleep, I returned to see the moon hovering over these giant rock spires, glowing in the predawn light. Despite the serenity of this image, it was actually quite chaotic behind the scenes, with temperatures hovering in the teens and wind gusts at thirty to forty miles per hour making it almost impossible to steady my tripod and adjust for the long focal length, as well as to apply a filter to temper the brilliance of the moon. Fortunately I was able to assess the scene quickly enough to note the moon's downward arc and that it would soon appear to be resting on the tip of this rocky outcropping.

*Composite image taken just outside Monument Valley Navajo Tribal Park.*

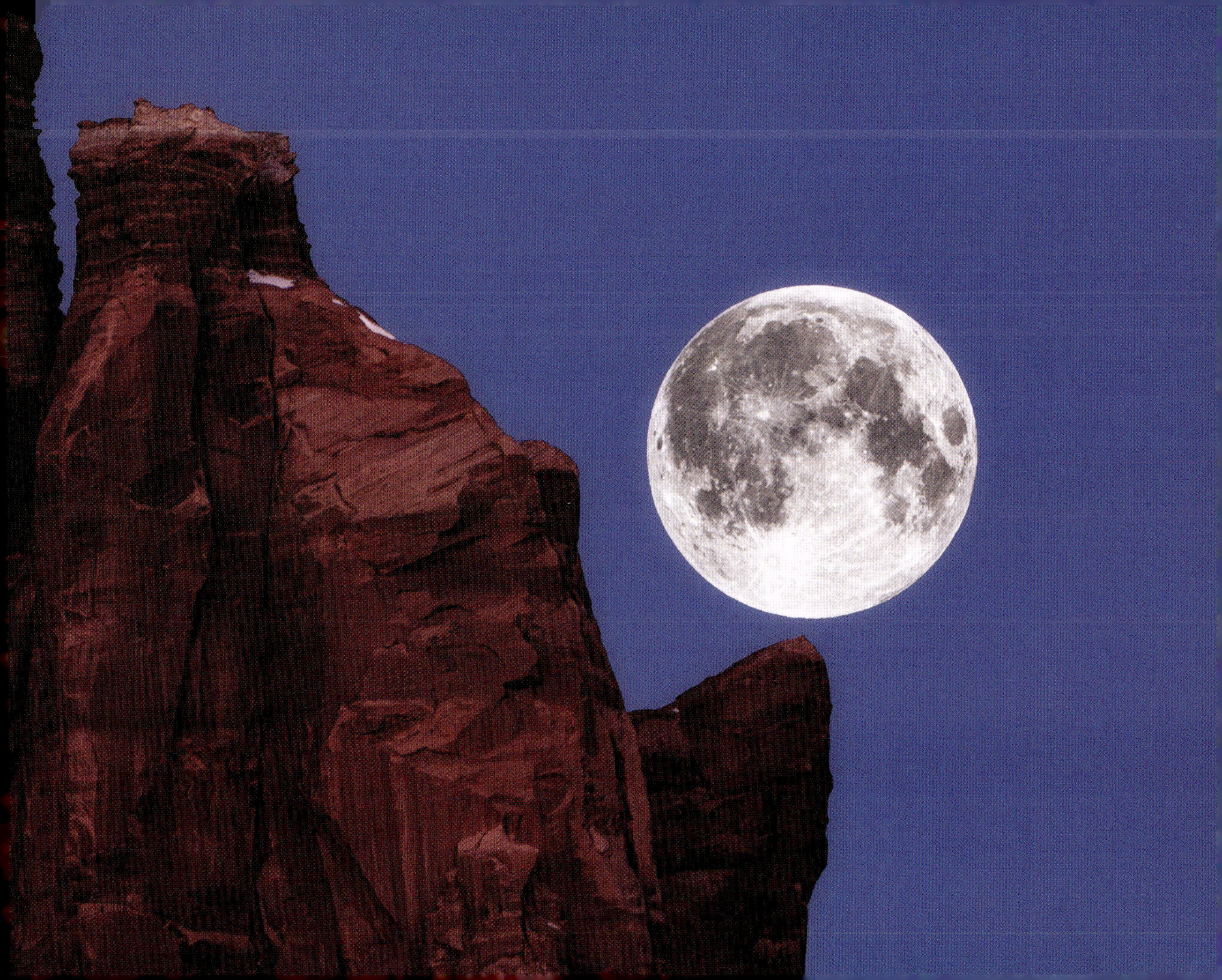

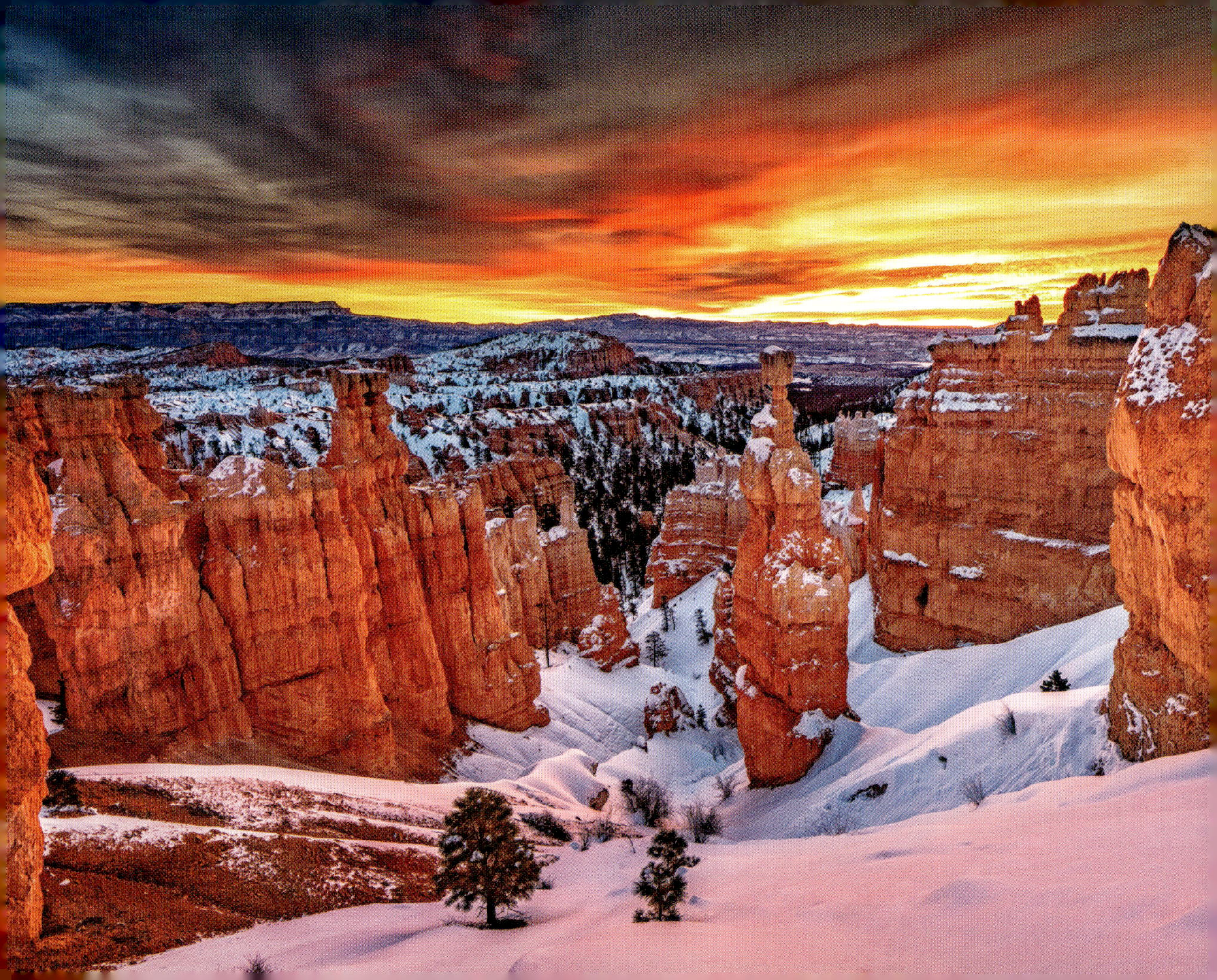

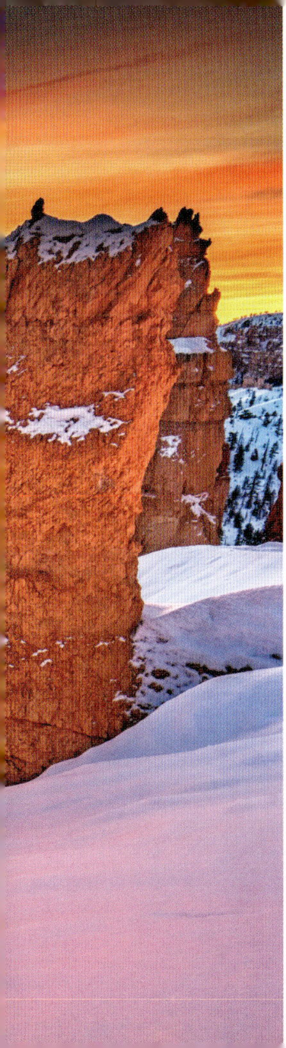

*Bryce Canyon National Park, Utah*

First it was ten locations. Then it was down to five. On a dim, snowy Tuesday morning at a Ridgway State Park campground in Colorado, I cracked my cold fingers and opened my laptop. After months of planning, five had now narrowed down to one: Escalante, Utah. Weather forecast: clear skies all day for Saturday, October 14, 2023. At 3 a.m. on Friday morning, I pushed off from Durango and made the seven-hour journey to Devils Garden.

I spent the morning scouting locations where the entire transit of the Ring of Fire eclipse would be seen, and I settled on this formation (affectionately now known in my mind as the Shark's Fin). The next day I arrived, made coffee, collected my gear, and walked off to begin. The few of us gathered here were enthralled as a brief pall was cast across the bright red soil and a chill descended. Our hushed awe turned to exhilaration, and cheers erupted across the strange, rocky landscape as the sun entered totality.

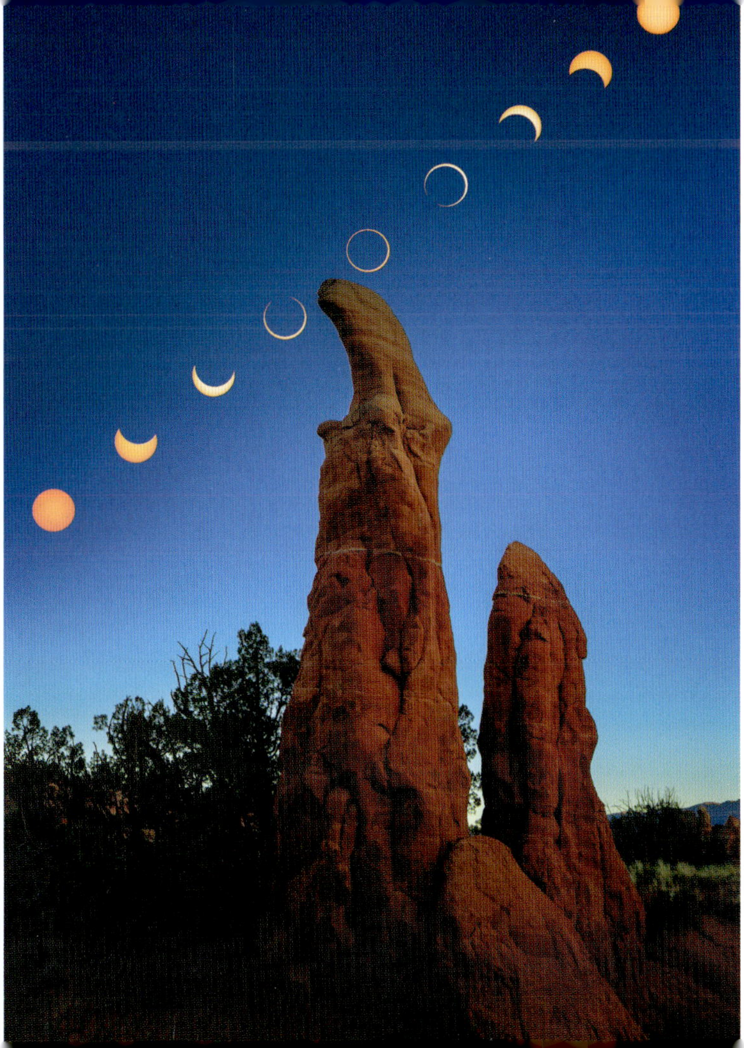

*Devils Garden, Grand Staircase–Escalante National Monument, Utah*

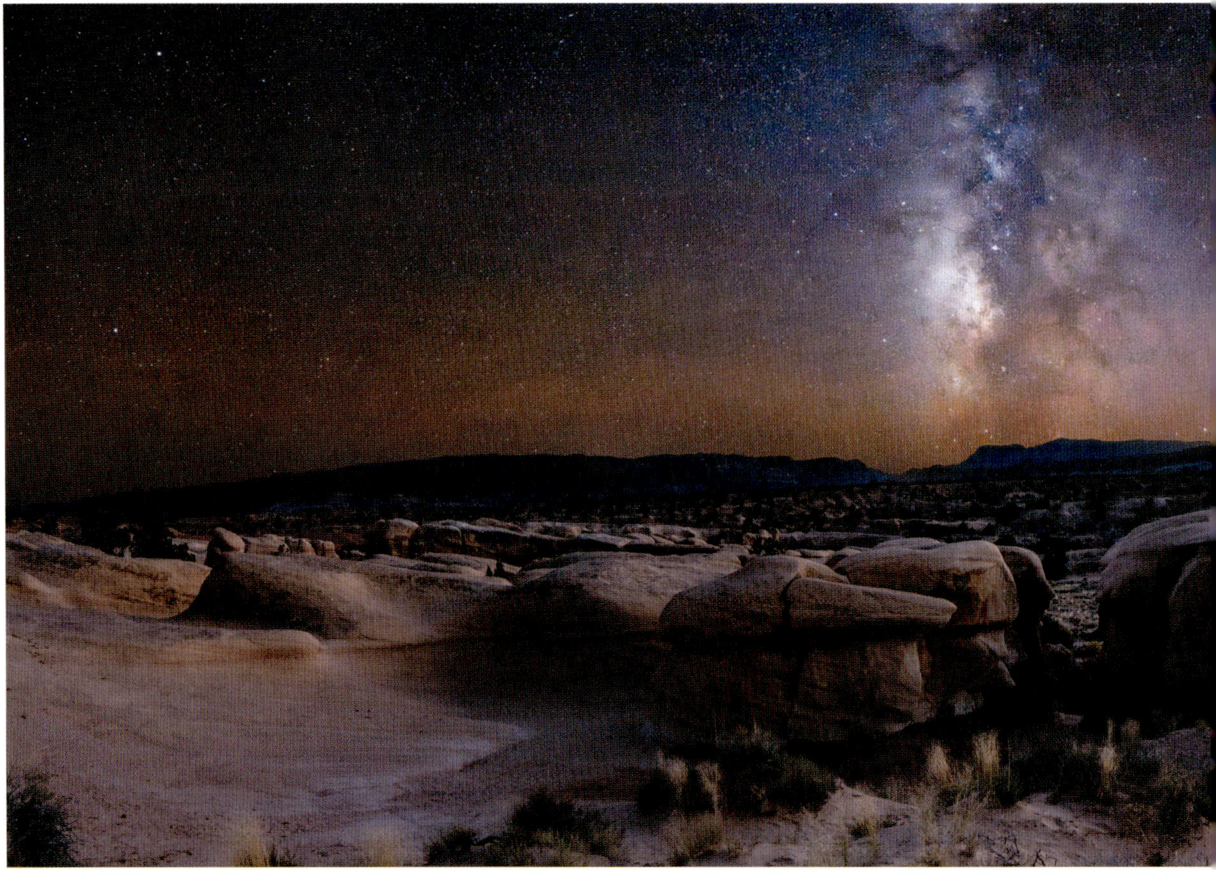

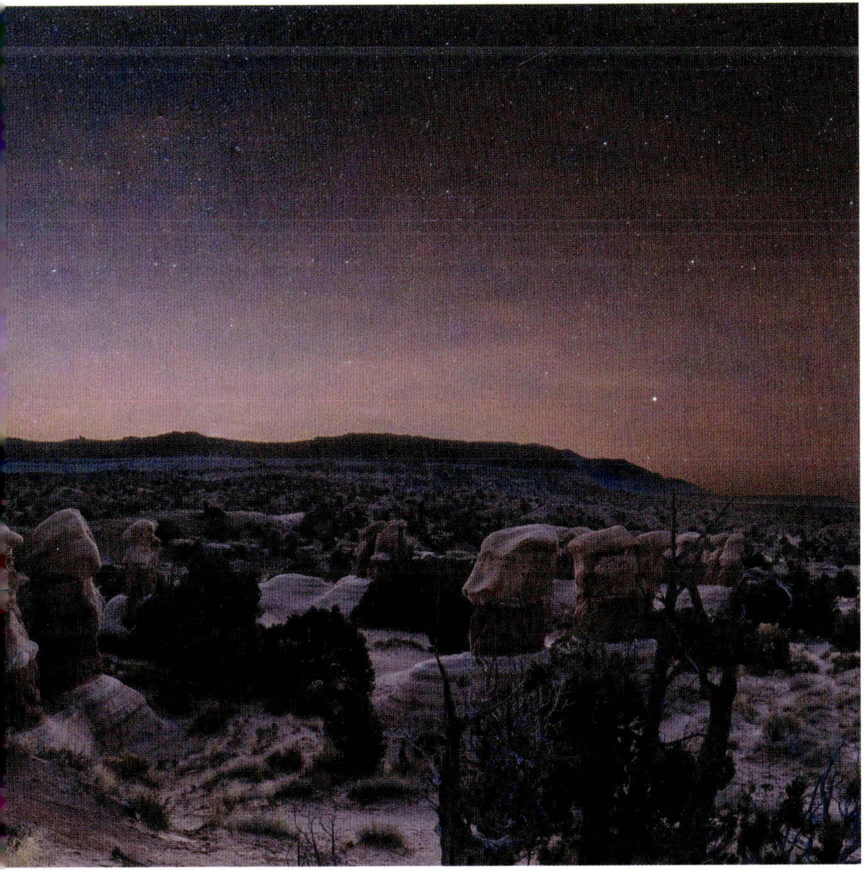

*Devils Garden, Grand Staircase–Escalante National Monument, Utah*

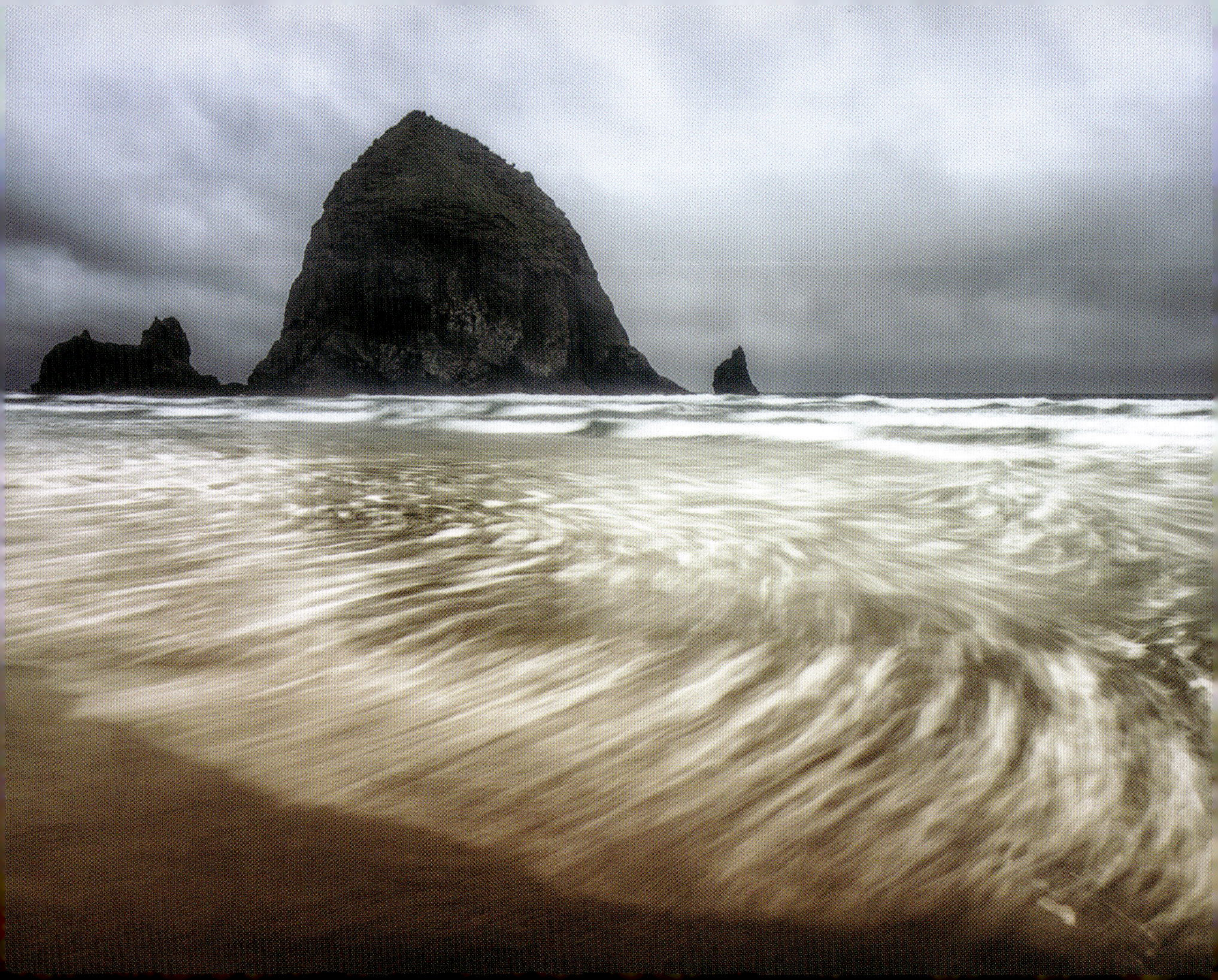

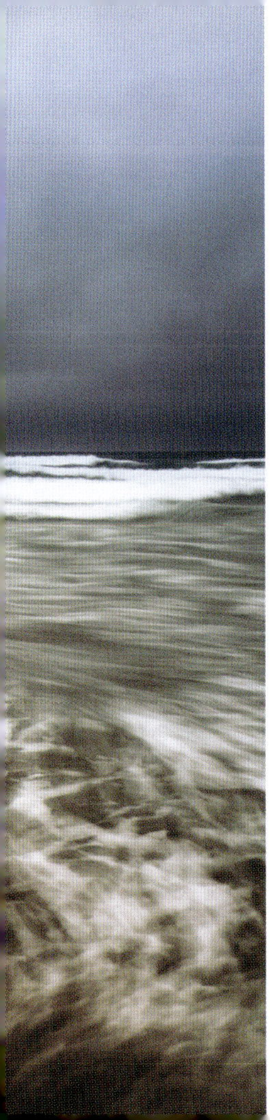

*Cannon Beach, Oregon*

*The lakes hidden among the hills are saints, and the sea too is a saint who praises God without interruption in her majestic dance.*

—THOMAS MERTON, *NEW SEEDS OF CONTEMPLATION*

Emerging from the woods near Second Beach at Olympic National Park reveals an otherworldly sight of haystack rocks and dramatic skies on an early fall evening. Make sure to bring a good headlamp for the treacherous climb over the giant logs and driftwood at the forest boundary!

*Olympic National Park, Washington*

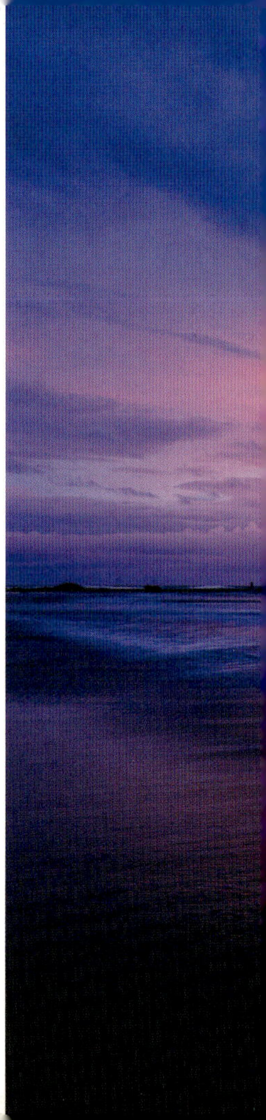

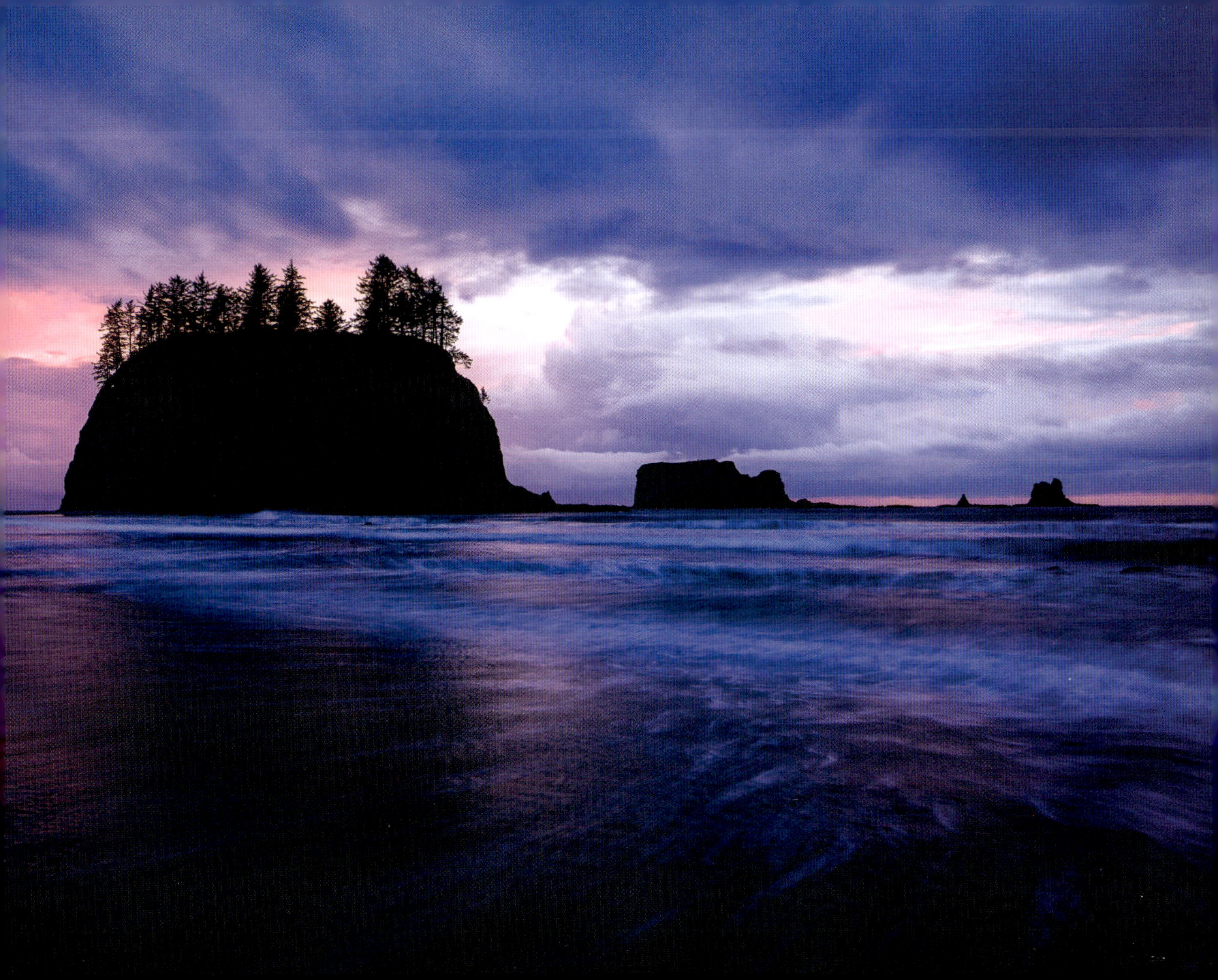

*There is a pleasure in the pathless woods,*
*There is a rapture on the lonely shore,*
*There is society where none intrudes,*
*By the deep Sea, and music in its roar:*
*I love not Man the less, but Nature more,*
*From these our interviews, in which I steal*
*From all I may be, or have been before,*
*To mingle with the Universe, and feel*
*What I can ne'er express, yet cannot all conceal.*

—GEORGE GORDON BYRON,
*CHILDE HAROLD'S PILGRIMAGE*

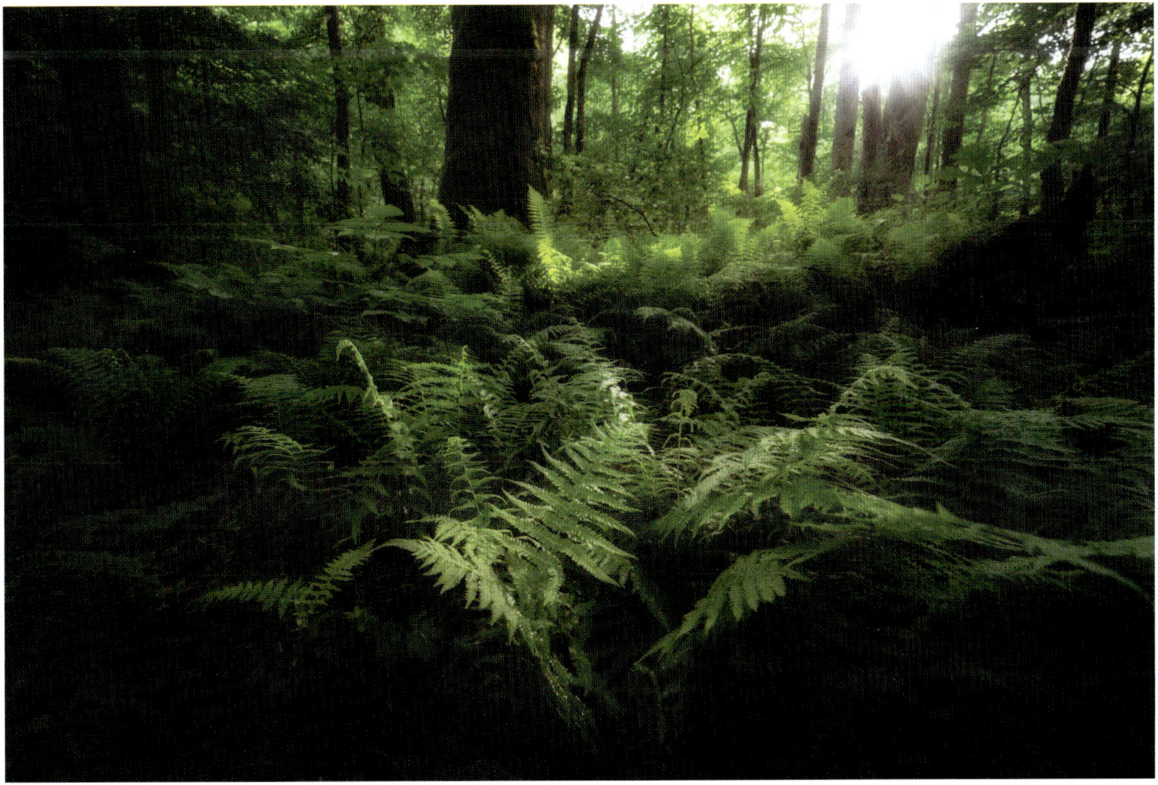

*Great Smoky Mountains National Park, Tennessee*

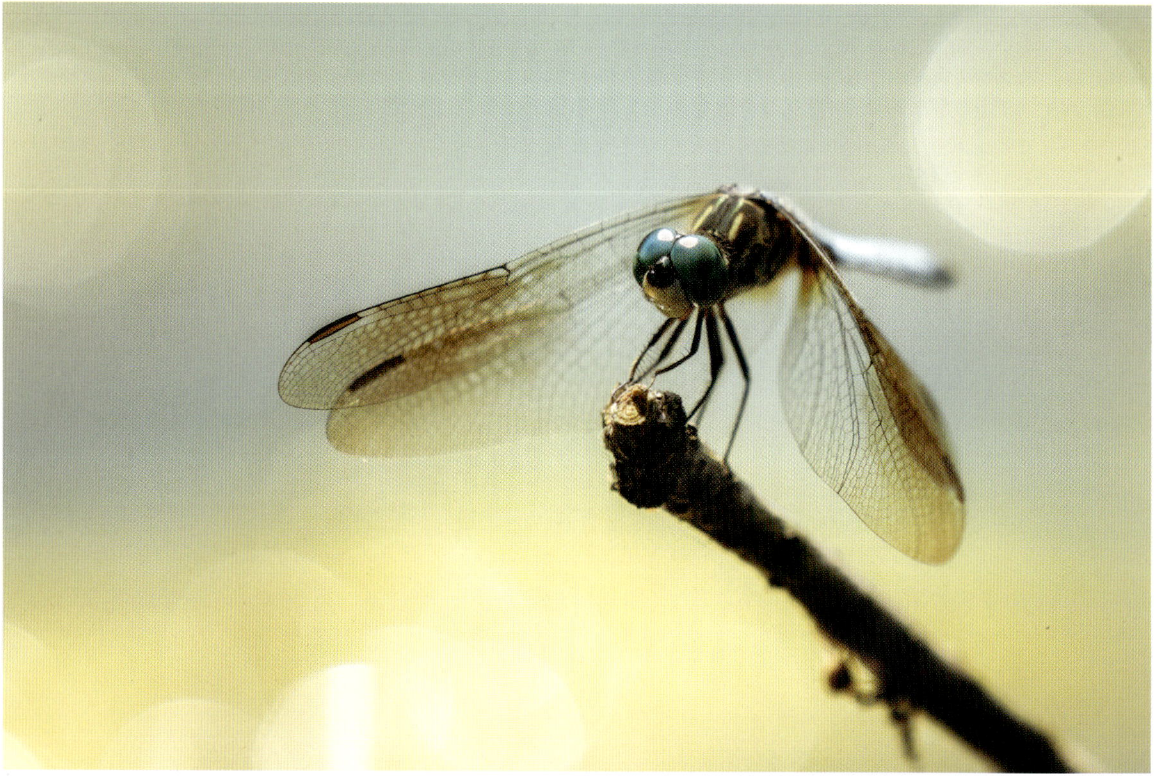

*Spring Grove Cemetery and Arboretum, Cincinnati, Ohio*

*When thoughts*
*Of the last bitter hour come like a blight*
*Over thy spirit, [. . .]*
*Go forth, under the open sky, and list*
*To Nature's teachings, while from all around—*
*Earth and her waters, and the depths of air—*
*Comes a still voice—*

—WILLIAM CULLEN BRYANT, "THANATOPSIS"

My stepfather passed away suddenly at the end of June 2019. He was a photography enthusiast and had always been supportive of my development. For the remainder of that summer, I was unmotivated to venture out, so I stayed close to home and spent several days exploring historic Spring Grove Cemetery and Arboretum in downtown Cincinnati. It was enshrined in the mid-1800s and patterned after the cemeteries and arboretums of Paris, a quiet landscape where people could enjoy natural surroundings among the monuments to the dearly departed. Herons, geese, swans, and, yes, even dragonflies are constant companions here, reminding all visitors—including grieving photographers—that life must go on.

Along the Pacific Coast near Yachats, Oregon, is the geological phenomenon known as Thor's Well. A hole in the side of the cliff allows water to rush in and disappear in what seems to be a bottomless pit. It is most spectacular at high tide, but make sure to stand several feet back, as you will get an unexpected drenching!

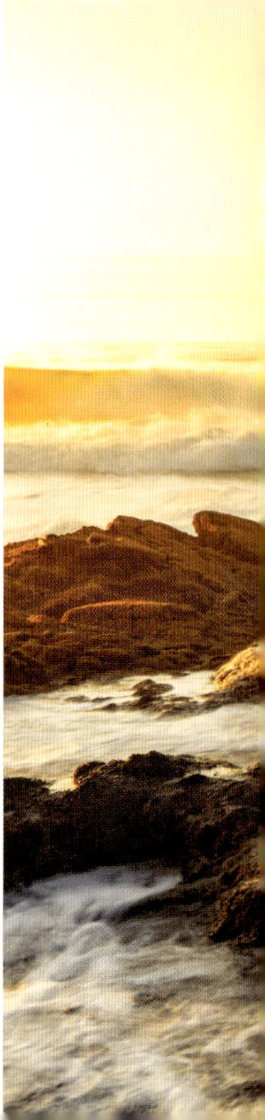

*Thor's Well, Yachats, Oregon*

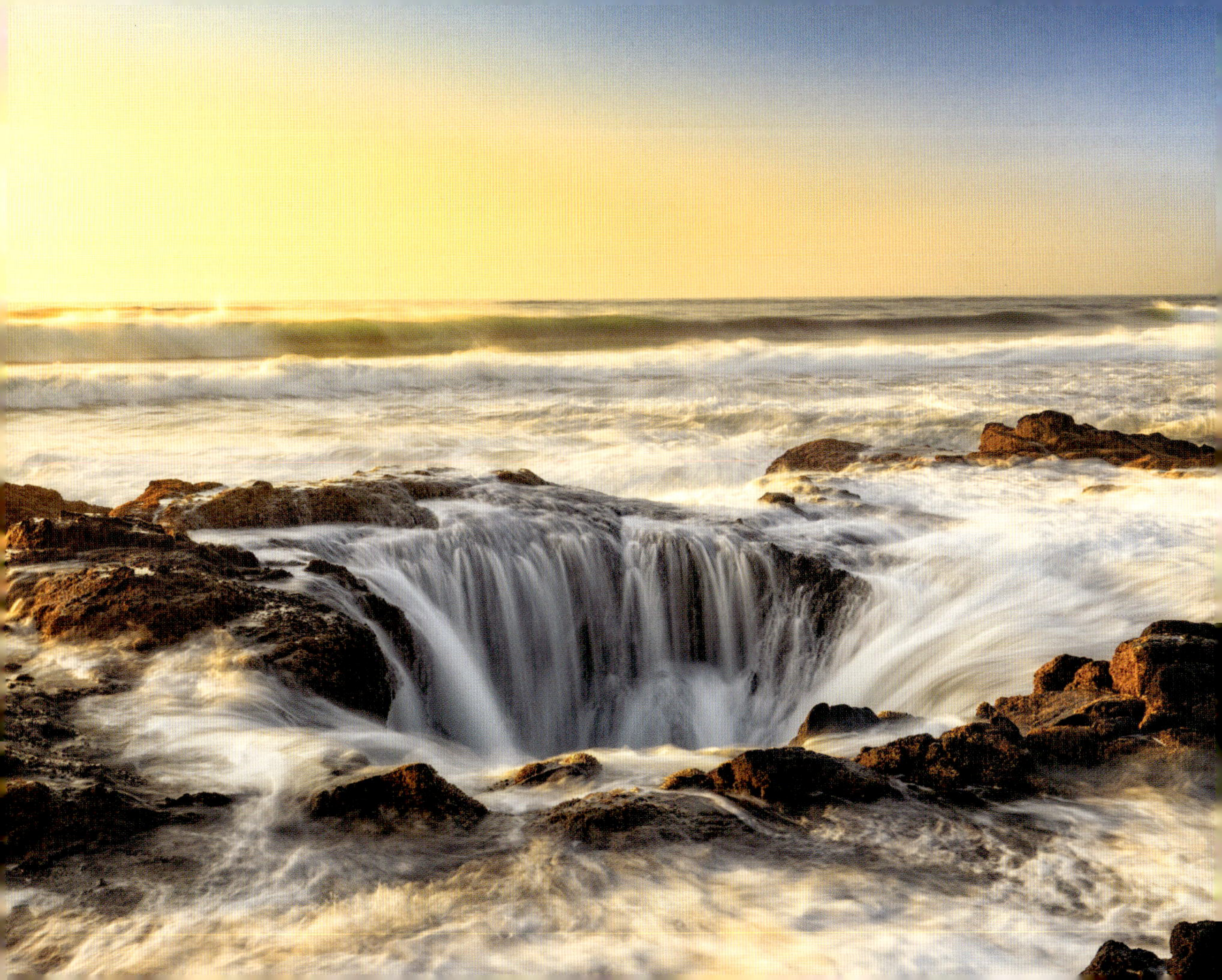

*Oh, earth, you're too wonderful for anybody to realize you. Do any human beings ever realize life while they live it—every, every minute?*
—THORNTON WILDER, *OUR TOWN*

As I explored the resplendent fall foliage along Shredder Falls in Cuyahoga Valley National Park on a blissful October afternoon, I came across this lone leaf, struggling against the current along the rocky shelf of Brandywine Creek. It held on long enough for me to examine its precarious state and contemplate compositional and light metering challenges before it dislodged and continued on, buffeted along its watery course and eventually reaching the swirling pool at the bottom of the steps of shale. I briefly noted its departure before moving back up the falls. The sun's rays would eventually shift and soon I had to return back up the trail.

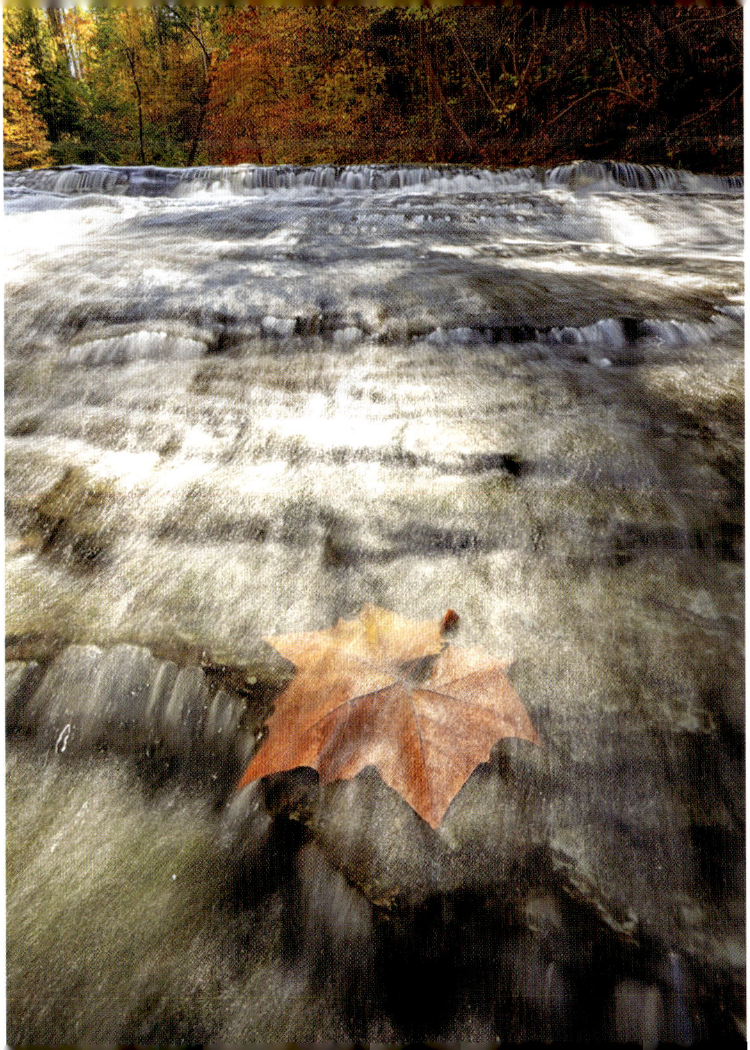

*Cuyahoga Valley National Park, Ohio*

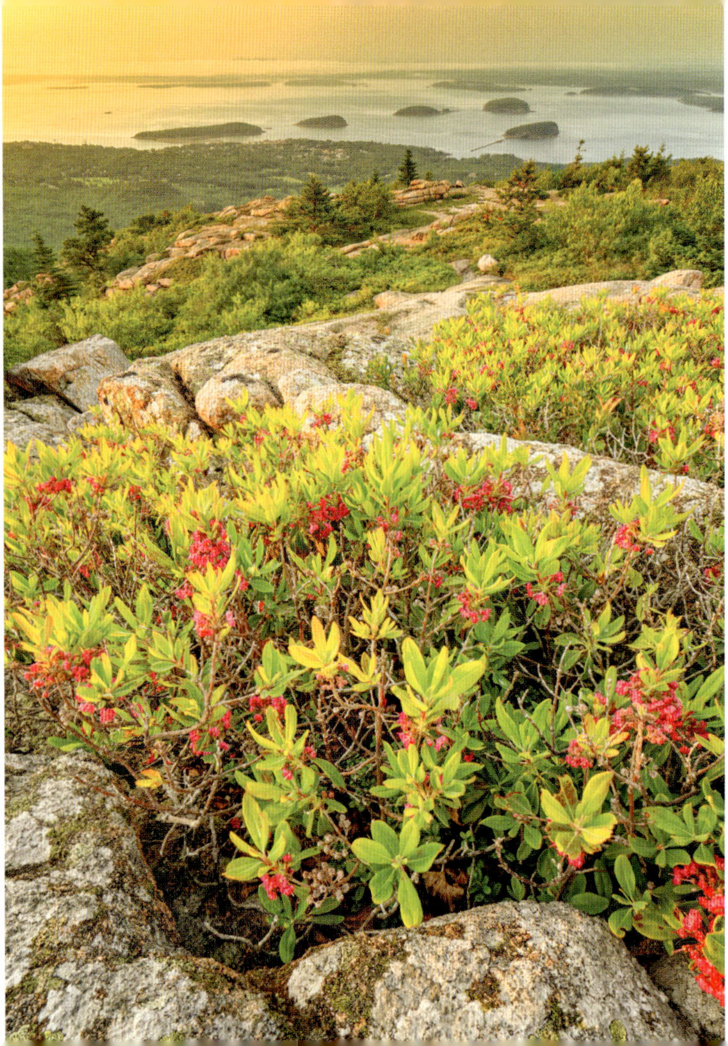

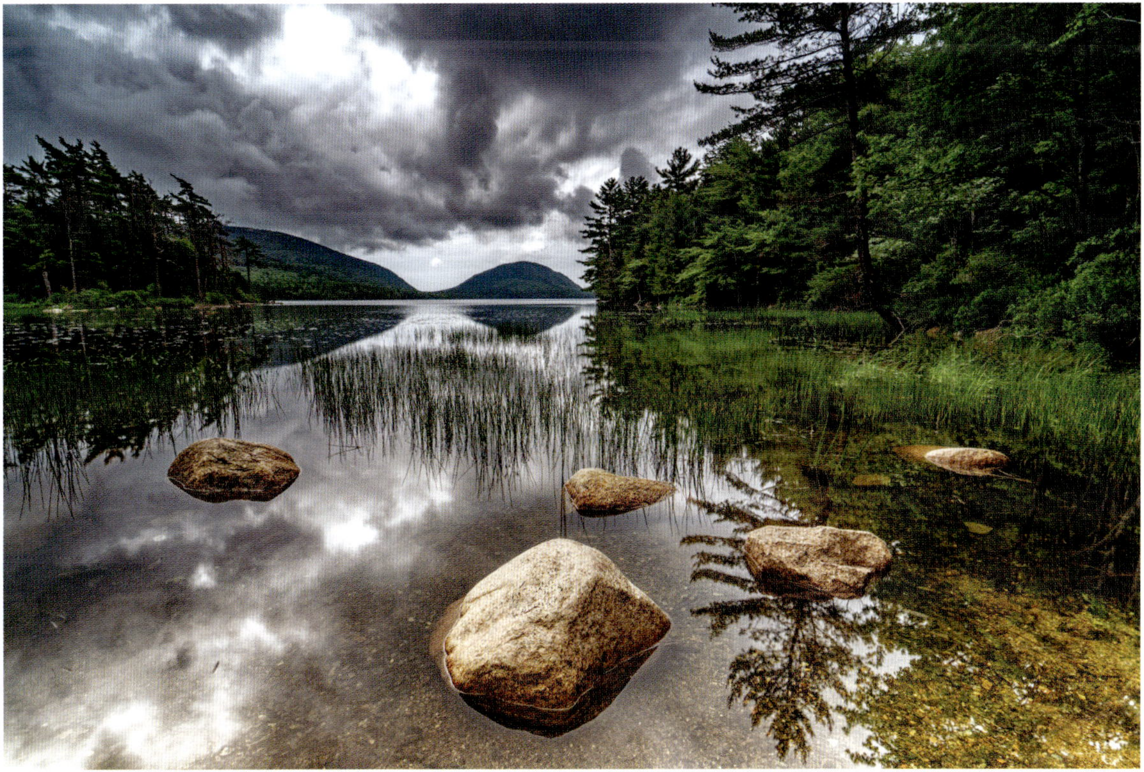

Left and right: *Acadia National Park, Maine*

I entered Crater Lake National Park at around 4 a.m. and immediately felt swallowed up by the nearly ten-foot snow walls lining the windy drive. It had been meticulously plowed, leaving me with the feeling that I was heading up the wrong way on a bobsled run. Fortunately, the gate entrance to Rim Drive had been cleared up to the visitor center, leaving just a hundred feet or so to this vantage point. Though capturing this scene at dawn had long been a dream of mine, that morning a greater thrill took place: I was able to climb up the giant snow mound from the parking lot without losing either snowshoe once!

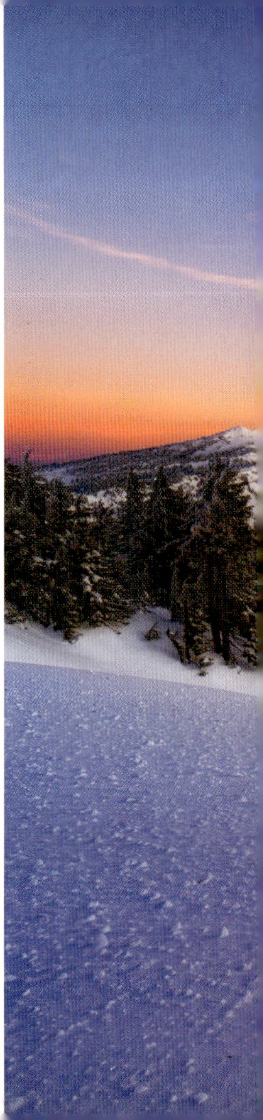

*Crater Lake National Park, Oregon*

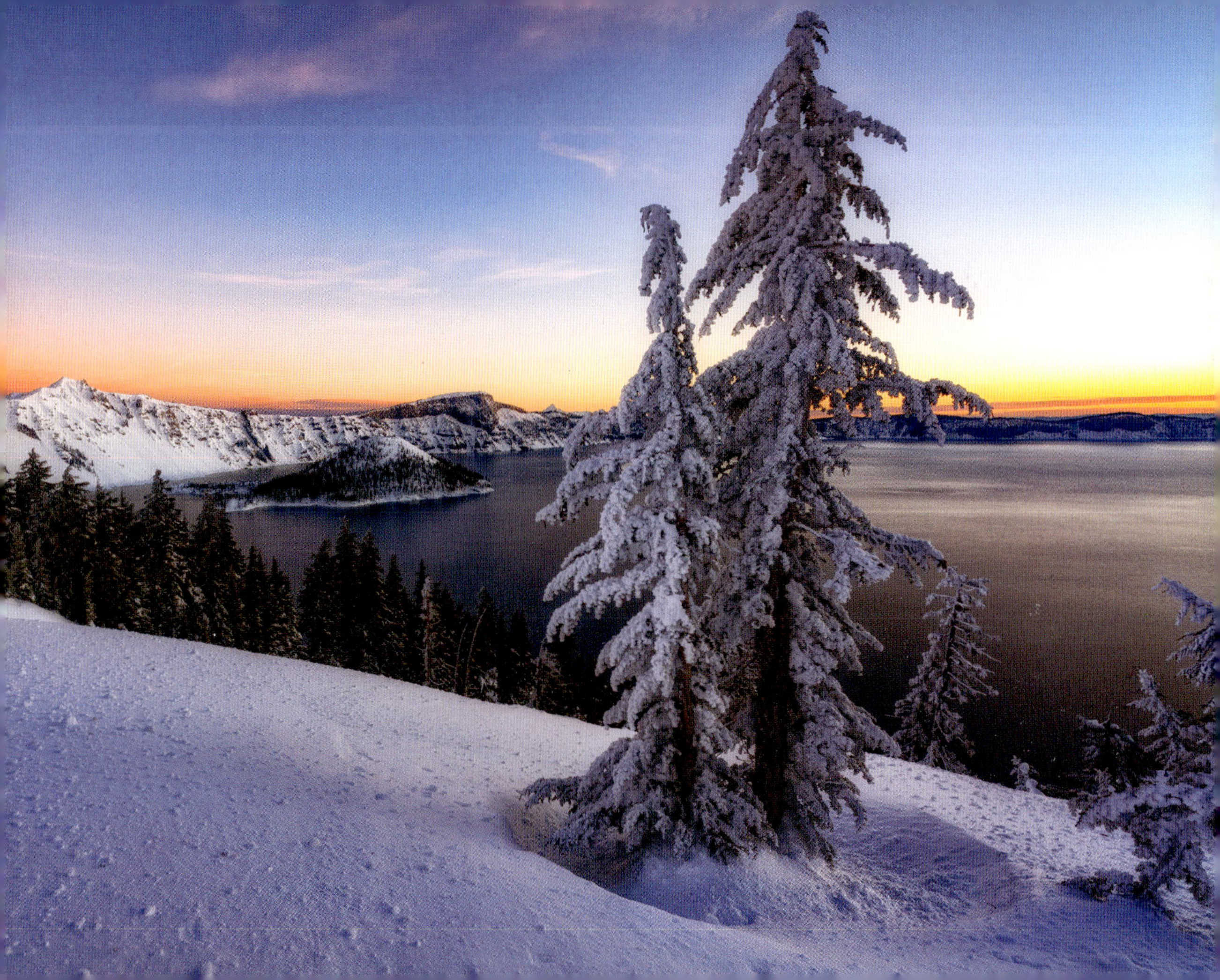

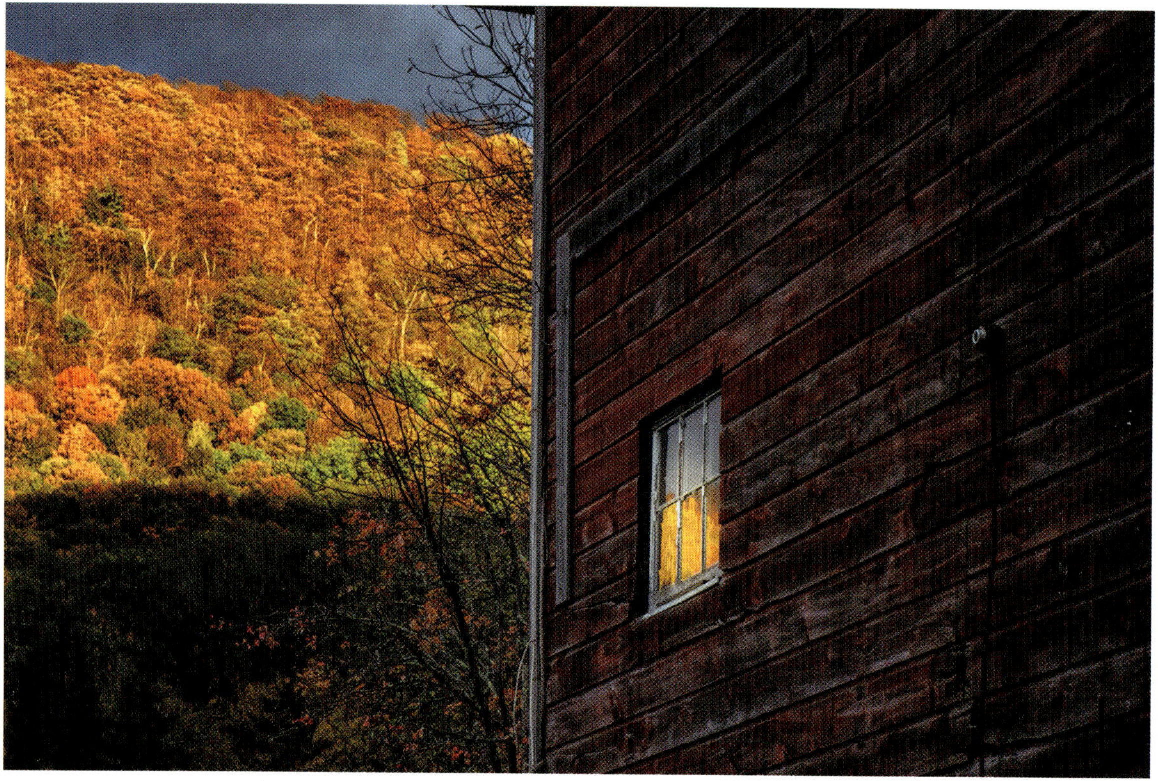

*Middletown Springs, Vermont*

*And at once the vicissitudes of life had become indifferent to me, its disasters innocuous, its brevity illusory—this new sensation having had on me the effect which love has of filling me with a precious essence; or rather this essence was not in me, it was myself. I had ceased now to feel mediocre, accidental, mortal. Whence could it have come to me, this all-powerful joy?*

—MARCEL PROUST, *IN SEARCH OF LOST TIME*

During the early autumn of 2020, we had the chance to visit some friends in central Vermont. It was my first time in the state, and I very much looked forward to scouting the idyllic countryside festooned in the colors of fall. Little did I imagine that my greatest photographic subject of that trip would be across the driveway.

A small barn, shabby but still intact, stood directly facing the front door of their farmhouse. It had become its own little anthropology museum, with remnants of rusty barrel rings and yellowed pages of old feed supply catalogs and calendars. As my friend opened the creaking door, the musty scents of old dried motor oil mixed with aging wood flooded me in a Proustian rush. Suddenly I was ten years old again, exploring my grandfather's farm, full of curiosity and blissfully unaware of the demands of the day.

The countryside could wait until tomorrow.

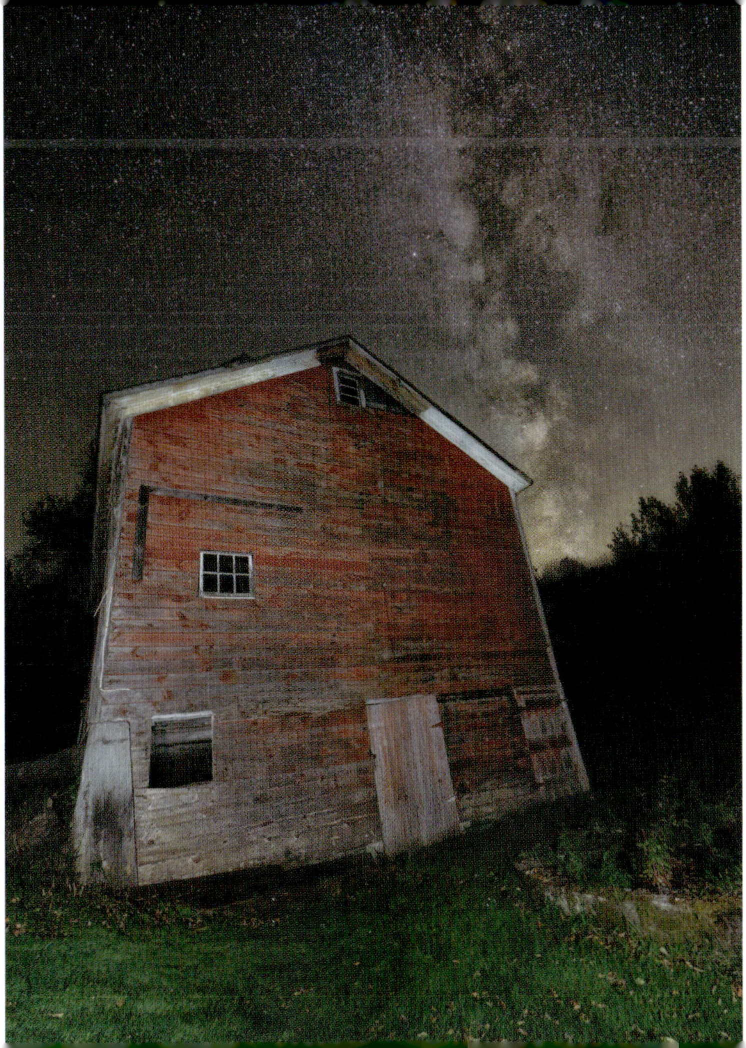

*Middletown*
*Springs, Vermont*

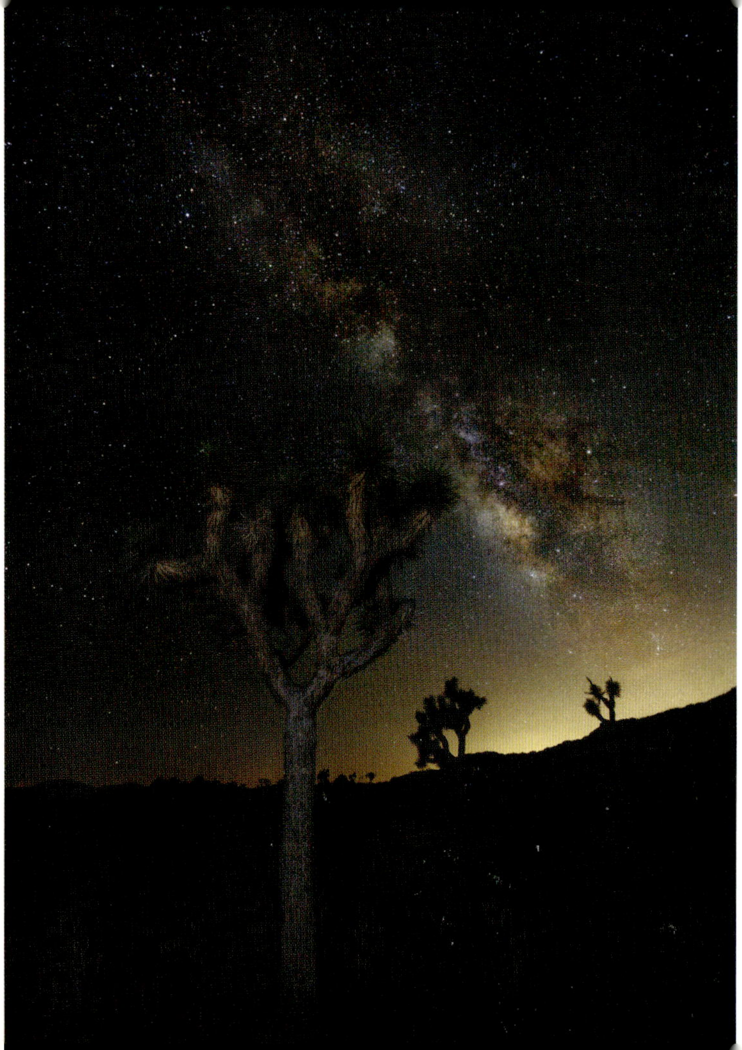

*Heaven and earth meet in Joshua Tree National Park, California.*

*The rays that come from those heavenly worlds, will separate between him and what he touches. One might think the atmosphere was made transparent with this design, to give man, in the heavenly bodies, the perpetual presence of the sublime.*

—RALPH WALDO EMERSON, *NATURE*

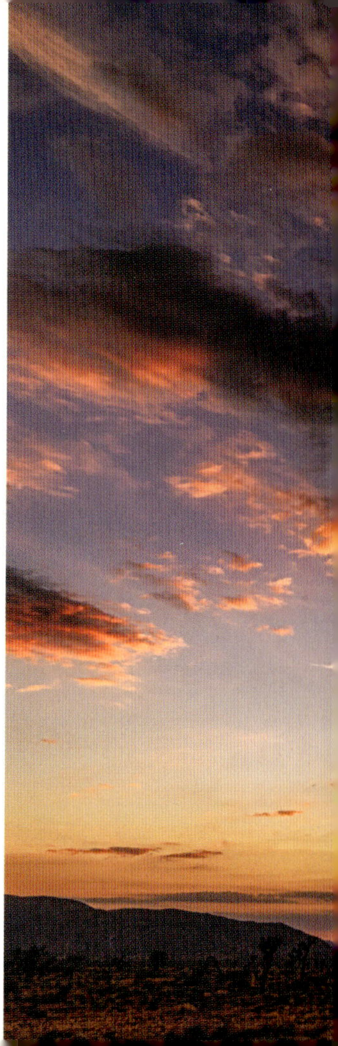

*Joshua Tree National Park, California*

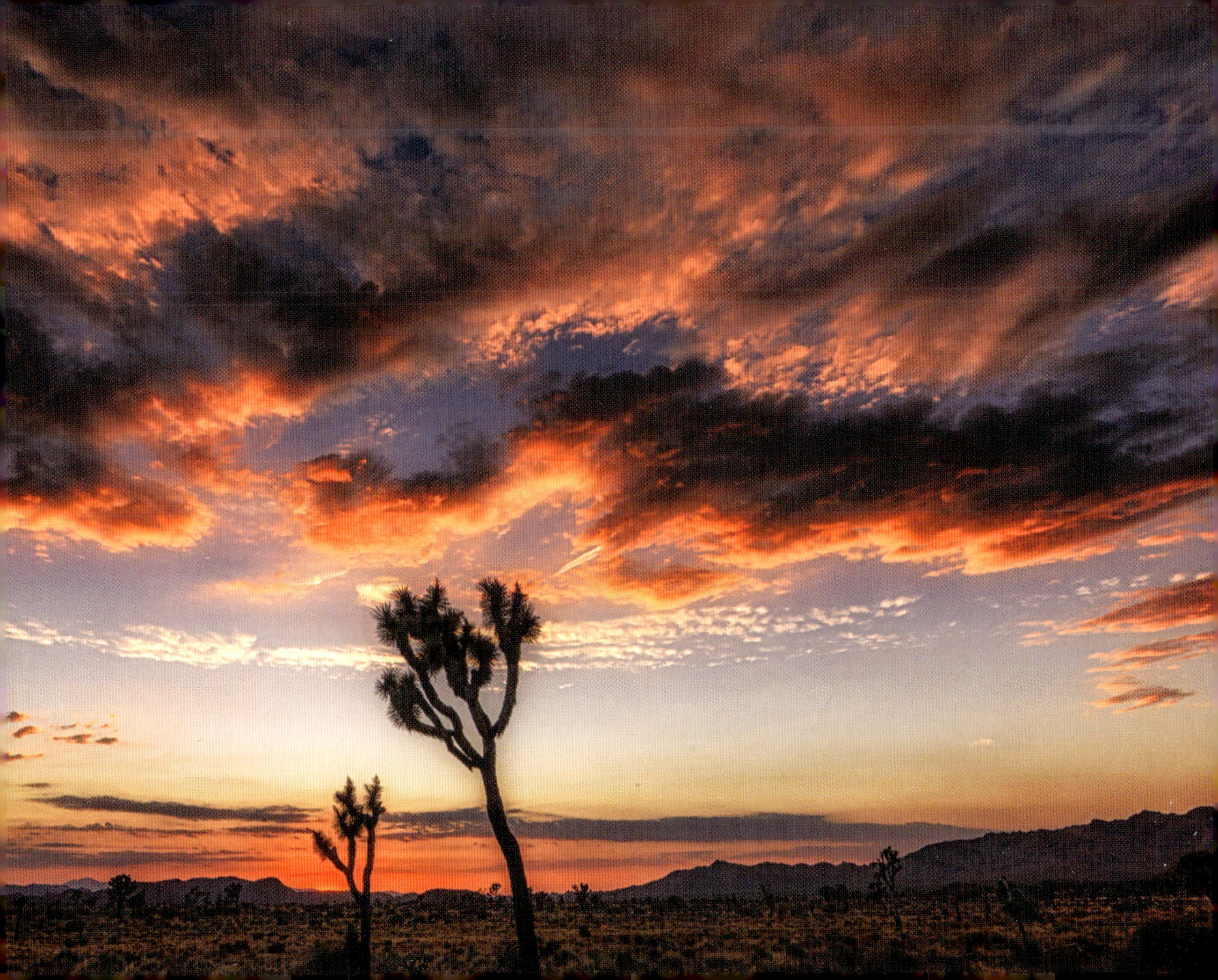

*There is an ecstasy that marks the summit of life, and beyond which life cannot rise. And such is the paradox of living, this ecstasy comes when one is most alive, and it comes as a complete forgetfulness that one is alive.*

—JACK LONDON, *THE CALL OF THE WILD*

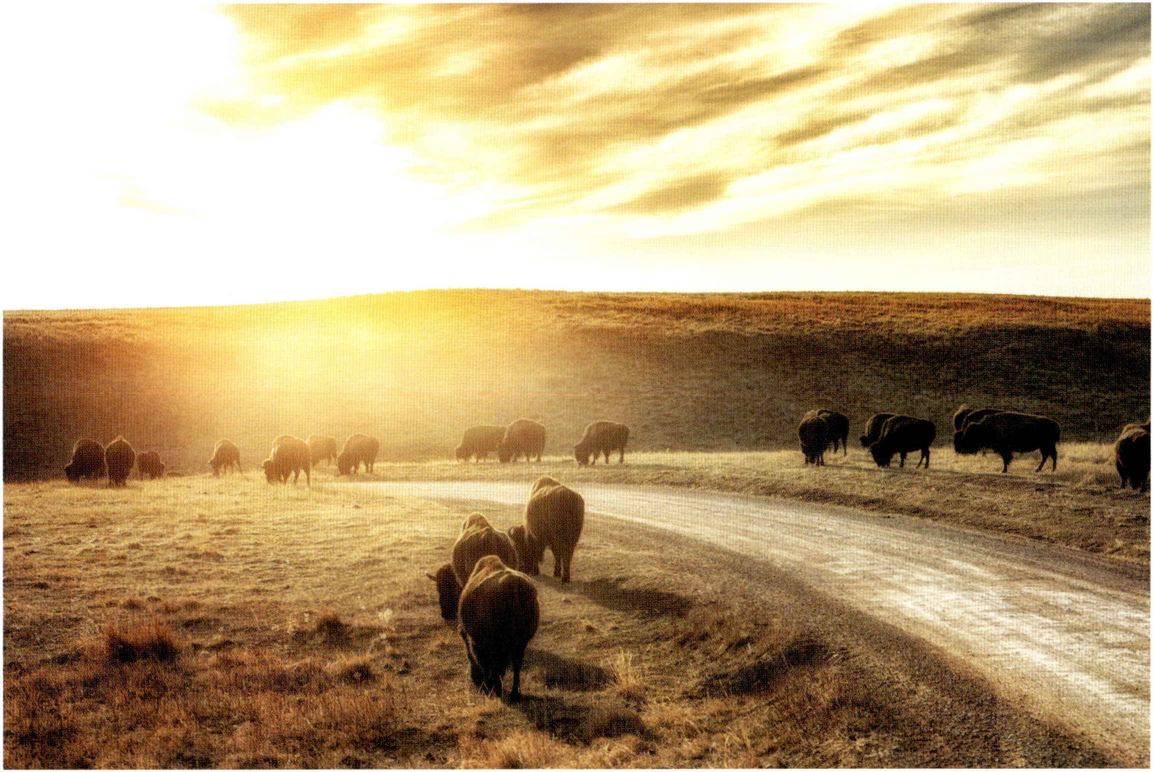

*Custer State Park, South Dakota*

It has lightly rained throughout the night in Gunnison National Forest, leaving the air fragrant with sage and my footsteps hushed on the soft, wet faces of fallen aspen leaves, looking up at me in quiet contentment as they began to recede under the arrival of those more recently departed. Aspen groves are often part of one giant root system, derived from a single seedling, and thus in life and now death they are still one. After one hour—or was it two?—I return to my car. Maybe I'll return tomorrow. Maybe I'll move on. I put the key in the ignition. The sun appears briefly among the swiftly moving clouds. Maybe it'll rain again. Maybe I'll stay . . .

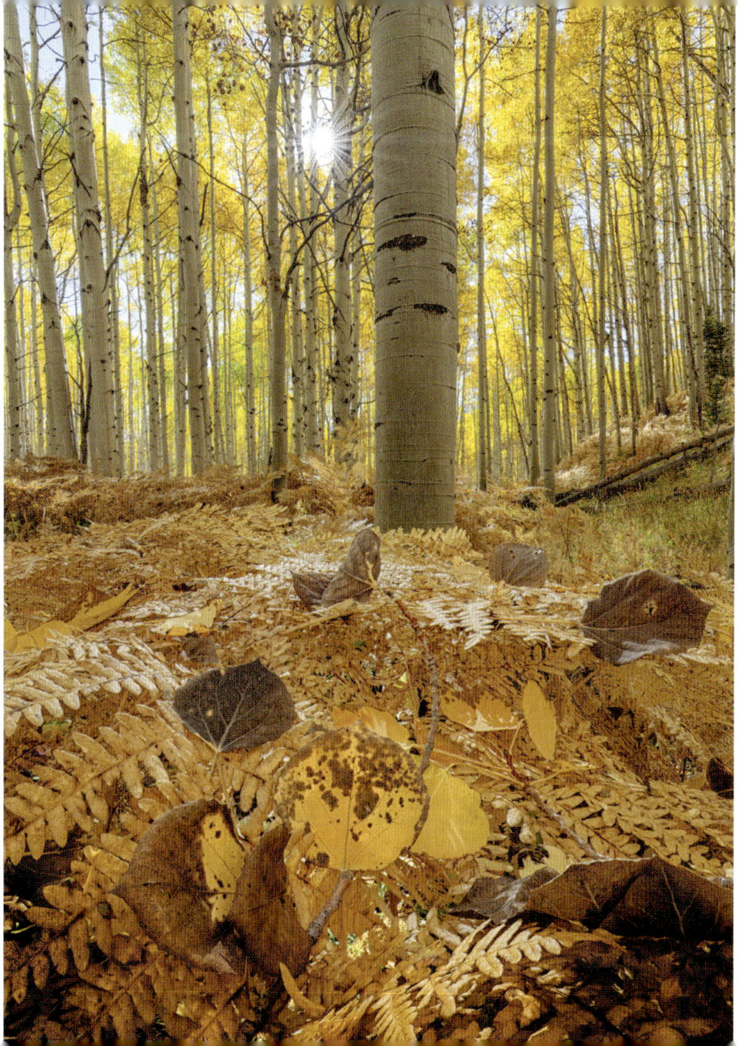

*Gunnison National Forest, Colorado*

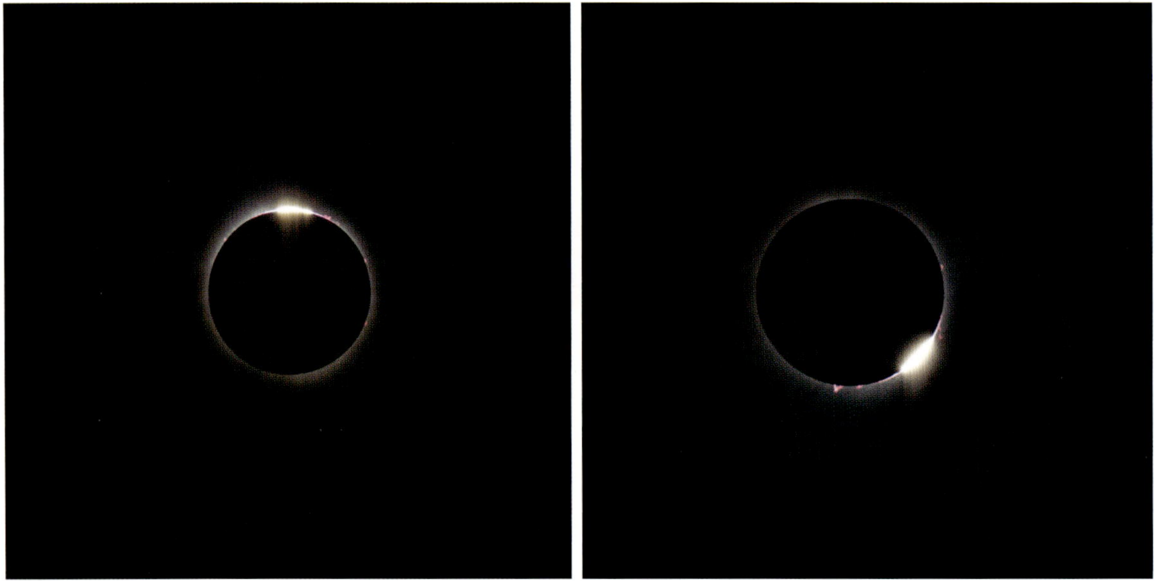

*Total solar eclipse captured at Pyramid State Recreation Area in Pinckneyville, Illinois, on April 8, 2024. Time of totality: 3 minutes, 41 seconds. Time of lasting memories: Forever.*

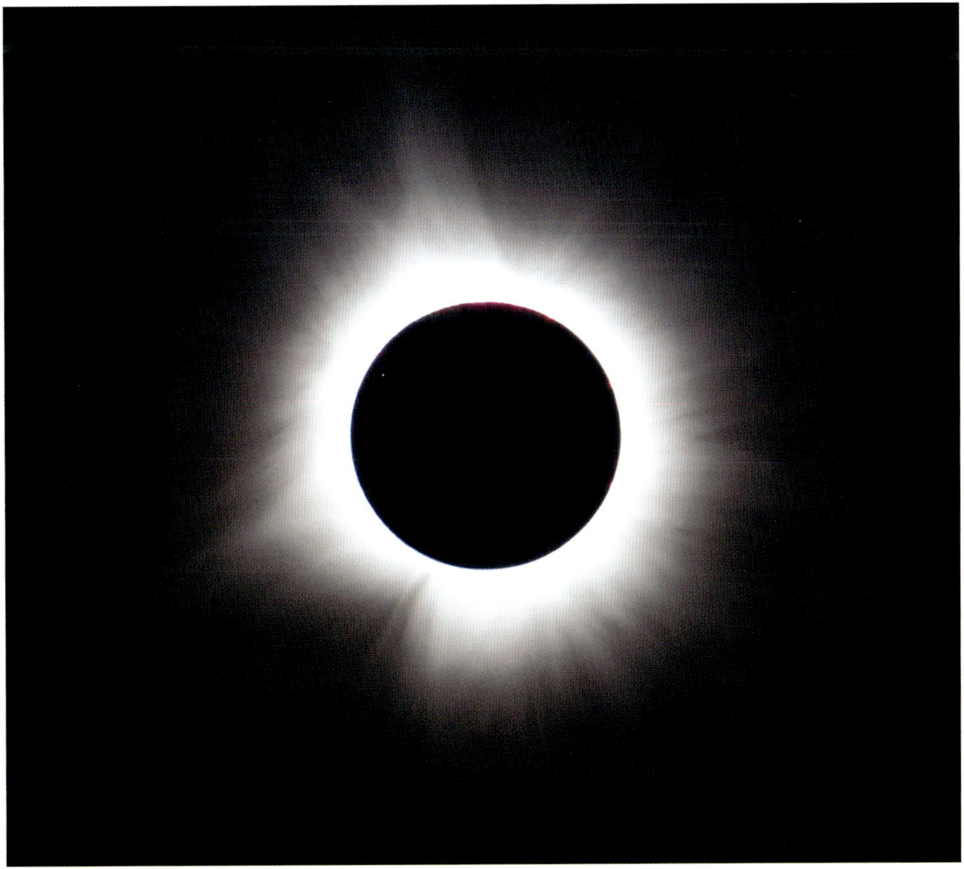

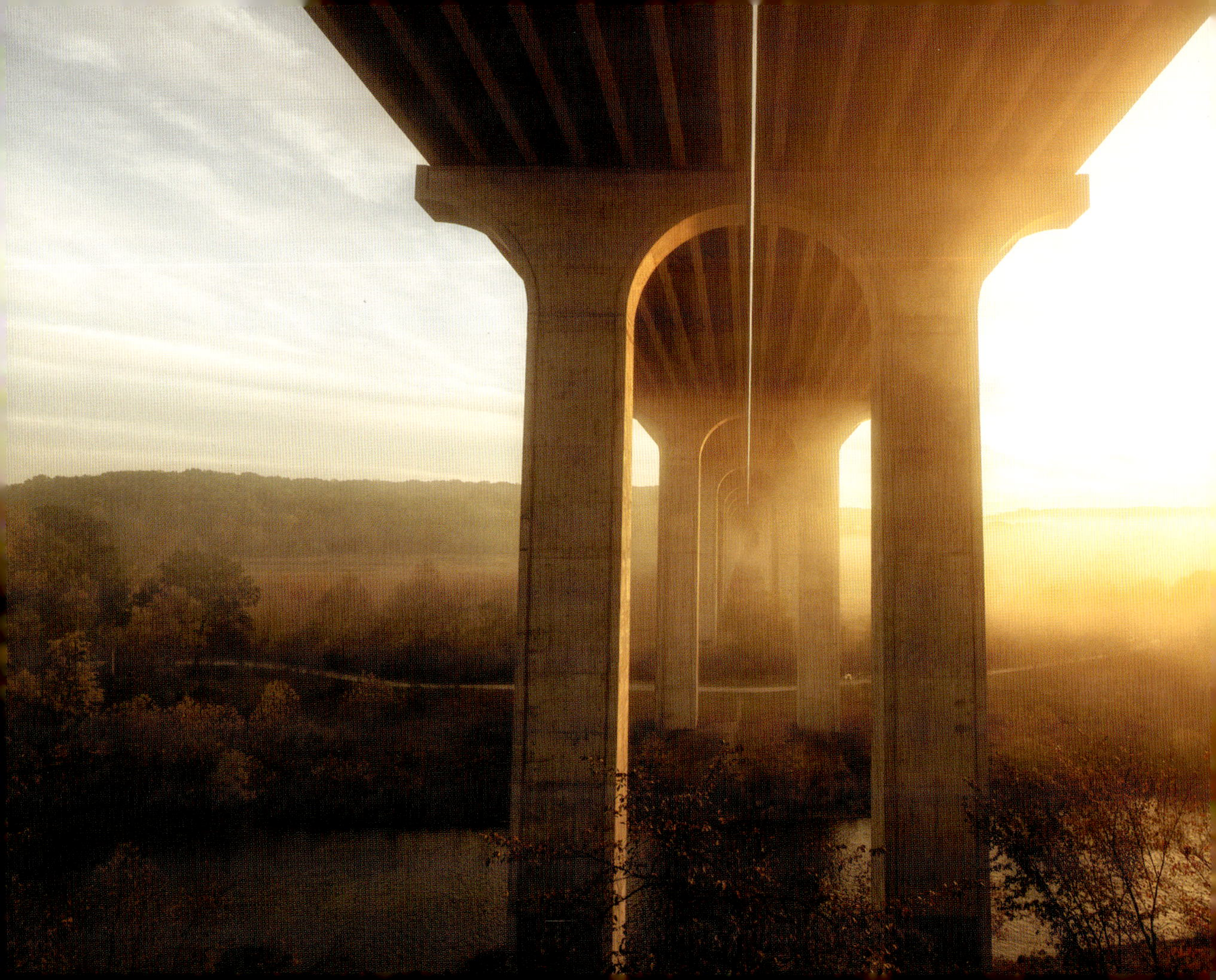

# Afterword

In an interview not long before his death, the famed landscape photographer Ansel Adams was asked to explain why he didn't use his work to advocate more directly for environmental causes. Even though he had been involved in efforts to preserve natural lands, Adams felt his primary obligation was as a photographer: "All the pictures I've done were done because I was there and I loved the mountains and I visualized a picture."

Adams saw the natural world as the source for human thought, much like Ralph Waldo Emerson had described almost 150 years before. It is perceived first visually and—more importantly—-emotionally, and only through deliberate observation and introspection can one begin to understand and later verbalize the process. For Adams, taking pictures of nature "is an intuitive sense and also an ability that comes from a lot of practice." The best he

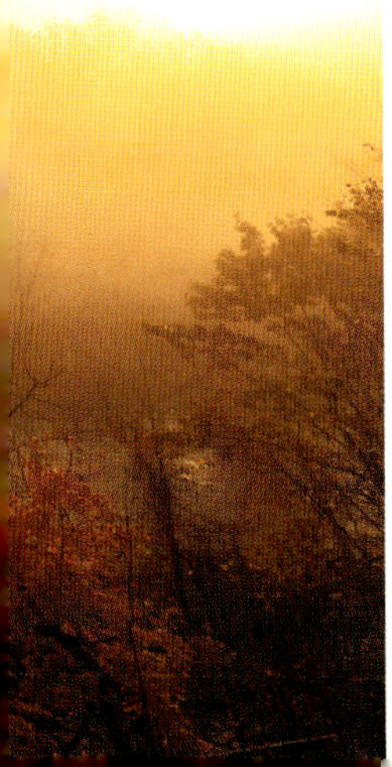

*Cuyahoga Valley National Park, Ohio*

could do would be to speak in the visual terms of his craft: form and texture, light and shadow, not in the flowery (or, in his opinion, didactic) language of nature writers. "You don't improve on nature," he said, you can only "reveal your impression of nature or nature's impact on you."

Forty years later, Adams's words perfectly describe my revelation that cold December morning. I had gone to that pond over and over again because I wanted to understand those geese and their behavior. Only after careful study, and a lot of trial and error, was I able to visualize a picture through the lens of my camera. In the process, I fell in love with photography and the natural world.

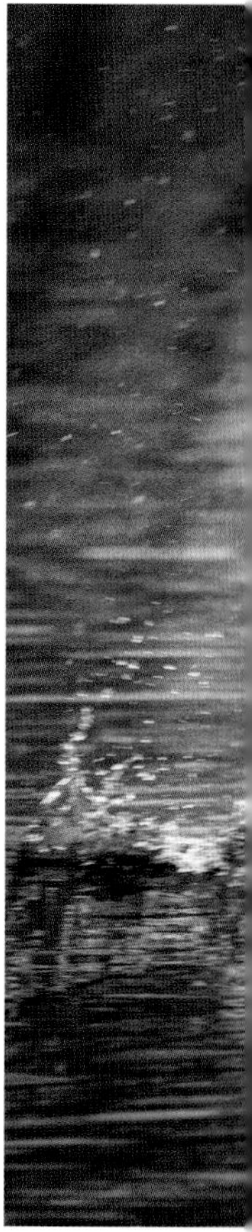

*A goose coming in for a landing at Spring Grove Cemetery and Arboretum, Cincinnati, in 2019.*

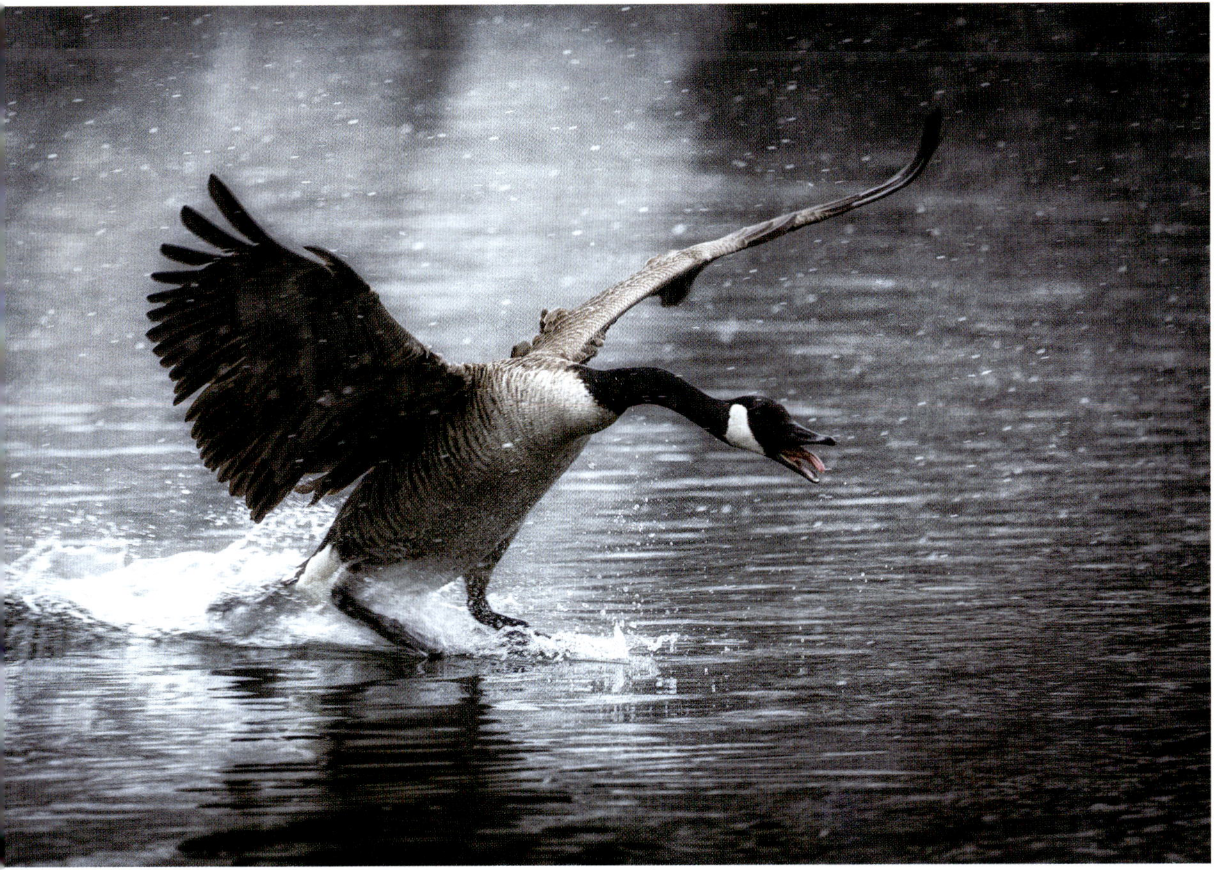

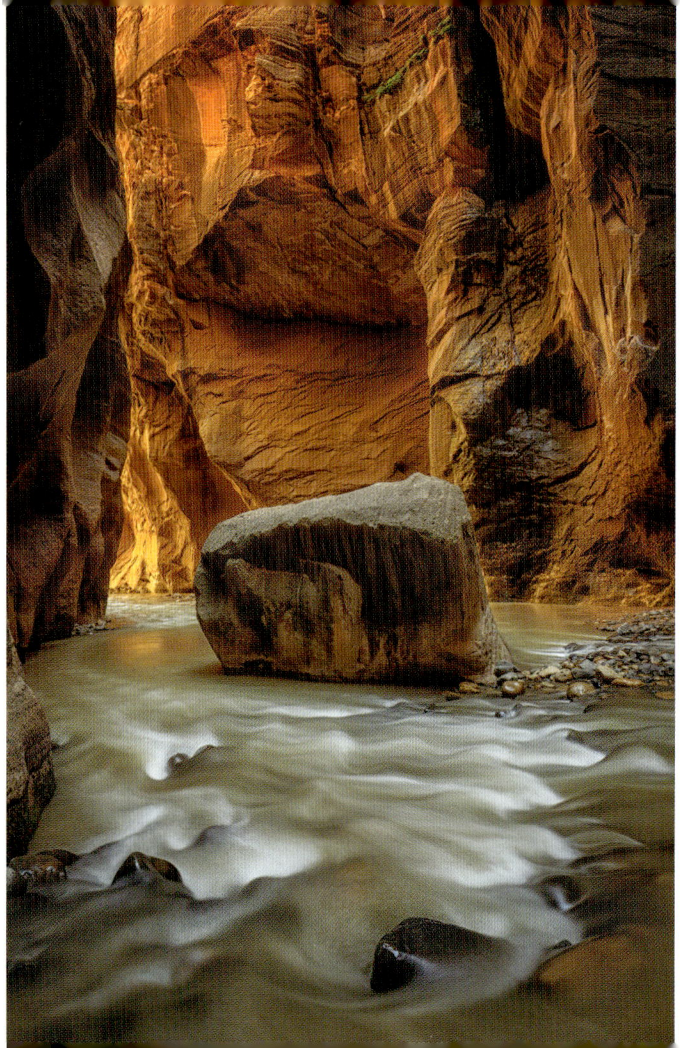

*Zion National Park, Utah*

# Eight Tips for Beginning Photographers

Photography began as a coping mechanism for me, a way to distance myself physically to seek an emotional space where I could make decisions and have a small measure of control over my life. Though I prefer to travel alone, I see myself as part of a larger photographic community. It is thanks to practitioners more skilled and experienced than I that I owe a large debt of gratitude, and I hope to pass on their knowledge and be a positive influence on those trying to learn the craft.

Here are some tips that helped me when I was starting out.

LEARN ABOUT THE CAMERA YOU HAVE: The smartphone has revolutionized what used to be called the "entry-level" digital camera market, so don't go out and buy a new camera if you are just starting out. YouTube can be an invaluable resource to learn all about your current device.

**FOCUS ON COMPOSITION:** It's easy to get overwhelmed by all of the choices available on digital cameras, such as ISO, focal length, shutter speed, etc. Focus on composition first and keep your camera on automatic settings, or use a preset setting, until you get more confident. Learn about basic compositional techniques, such as the "rule of thirds," and consider how to balance your subject versus the amount of negative space in the frame.

**BE INTENTIONAL:** Like with anything, you need to practice to improve. Set aside time and try different kinds of photography (macro, landscape, urban, etc.) to see what interests you. It's good to take many pictures in the beginning to gain confidence in your skills—but consider that the more pictures you take, the more you have to go through!

**MOVE YOUR FEET BUT WATCH OUT:** Zoom lenses or optical zooms can make us a bit lazy. Get closer to the subject and consider different angles or compositions—but remember to be respectful! Keep at least 75 feet away from wildlife and 300 feet from any large wildlife. Also, be considerate of your surroundings. The lure of the perfect selfie or Instagrammable moment has led to many unfortunate incidents.

**FRAME A SHOT WITHOUT YOUR CAMERA:** Sometimes we limit our photographic potential if we consider only what the shot will look like through our viewfinder or a screen. Take some time to scout a location or look at a subject first, and then examine it more closely through the lens. There might be compositions or angles that you didn't consider.

CONSIDER THE LIGHT: There is a reason photographers like to shoot during the "golden hour" before sunrise and sunset—the color temperature is more pleasing; the light is subtler and more evenly distributed across a landscape. Rainy days often help to add mood to a picture; overcast skies are perfect for shooting waterfalls or streams, especially in fall. Midday light can often be harsh and cause extreme shadows, so try to avoid areas of high contrast and, if possible, keep the sun behind you (unless shooting a portrait or group photo—you don't want the people squinting).

BACK UP YOUR PHOTOS: Don't just keep them on a flash card or device or even a computer. Have at least one backup hard drive, and consider printing out the pictures you would like to keep.

ENJOY THE PROCESS: Everyone wants a great shot, but the process of getting there will take time. I like to call it "serious fun" when you are focused on the task at hand but also taking time to enjoy what you are learning. Also, it's perfectly fine to study others' work to learn about the process and even imitate them in the beginning. Eventually you will begin to develop your own visual style.

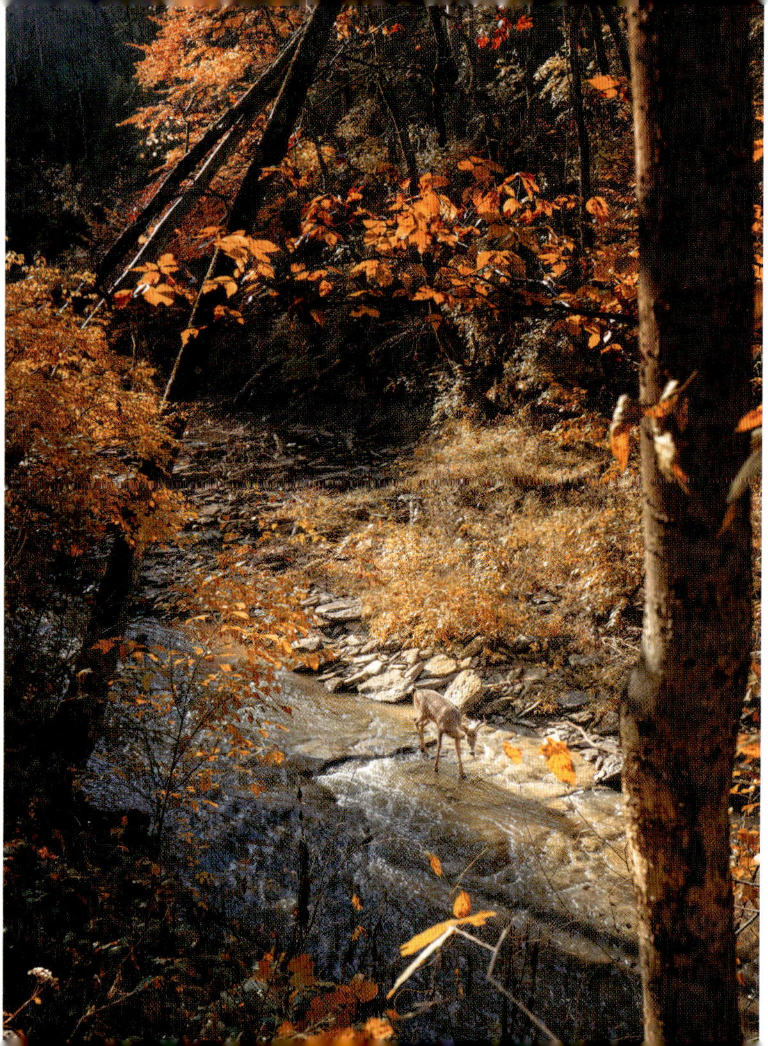

*A lone deer in Sharon Woods Gorge, Sharonville, Ohio, a favorite local spot.*

# Acknowledgments

I want to thank the entire Countryman Press team, especially Ann Treistman and Anne Somlyo, for their enthusiasm for this project from the beginning. The final result is beyond my wildest dreams.

I would also like to thank my editor, Aurora Bell, for her support and direction. Her patience and clarity were invaluable in guiding this novice through his first manuscript.

To Joe Thomas, a great photography instructor based out of Colorado, for his insight and inspiration and for getting me to think beyond being just a hobbyist.

To my parents, for their support over the years in all of my attempts at artistic pursuits.

Finally, to my wife, Jen, for encouraging me to hit the road and letting me see where it would lead. This never would have been possible without you.

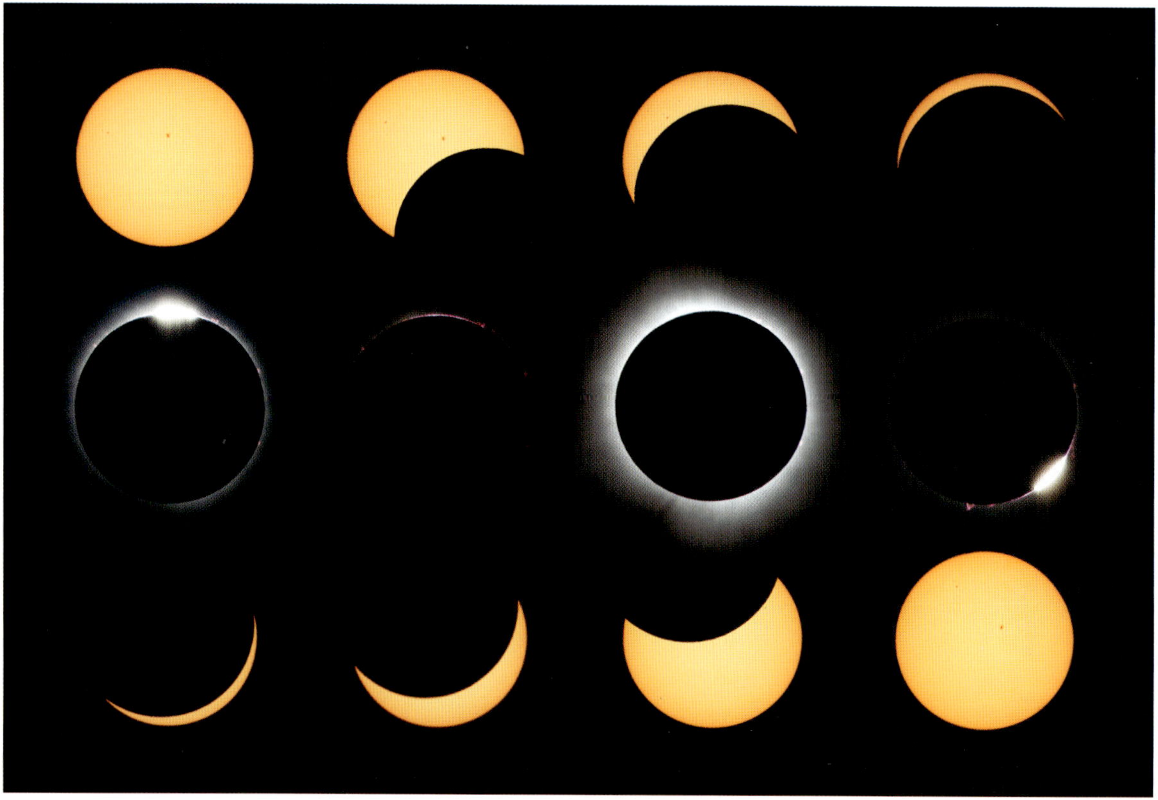

*Pyramid State Recreation Area, Pinckneyville, Illinois, April 8, 2024*

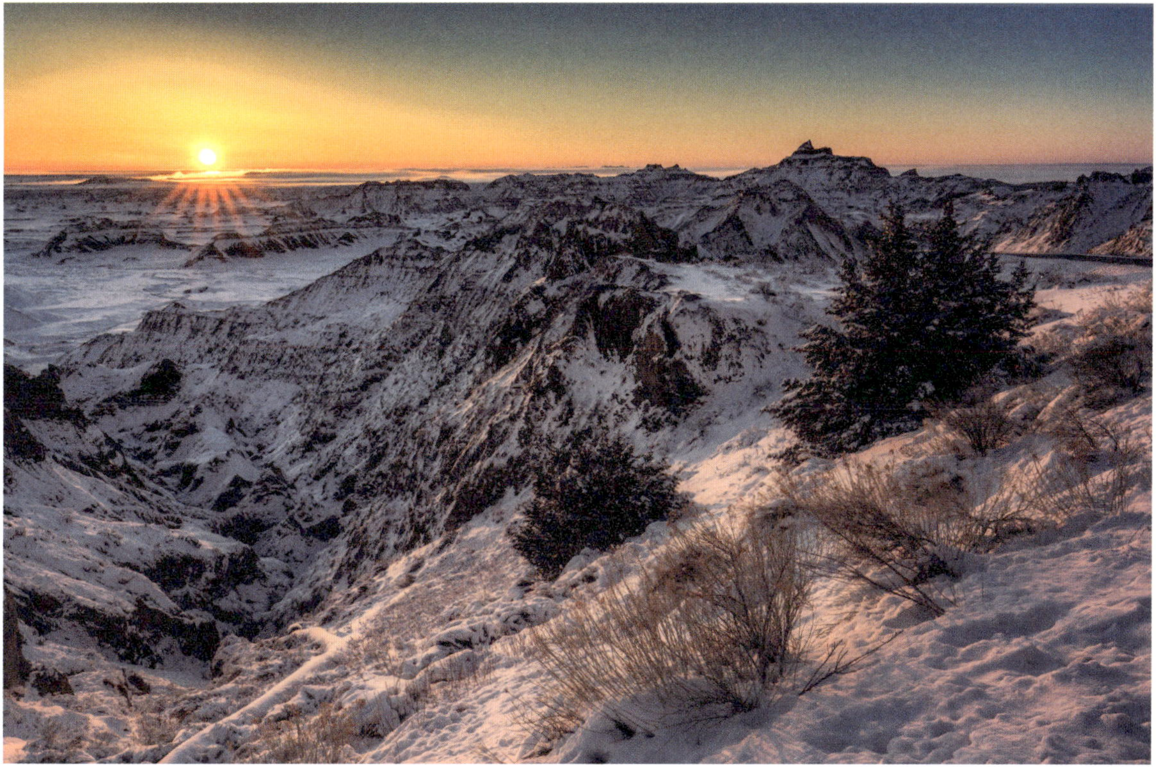

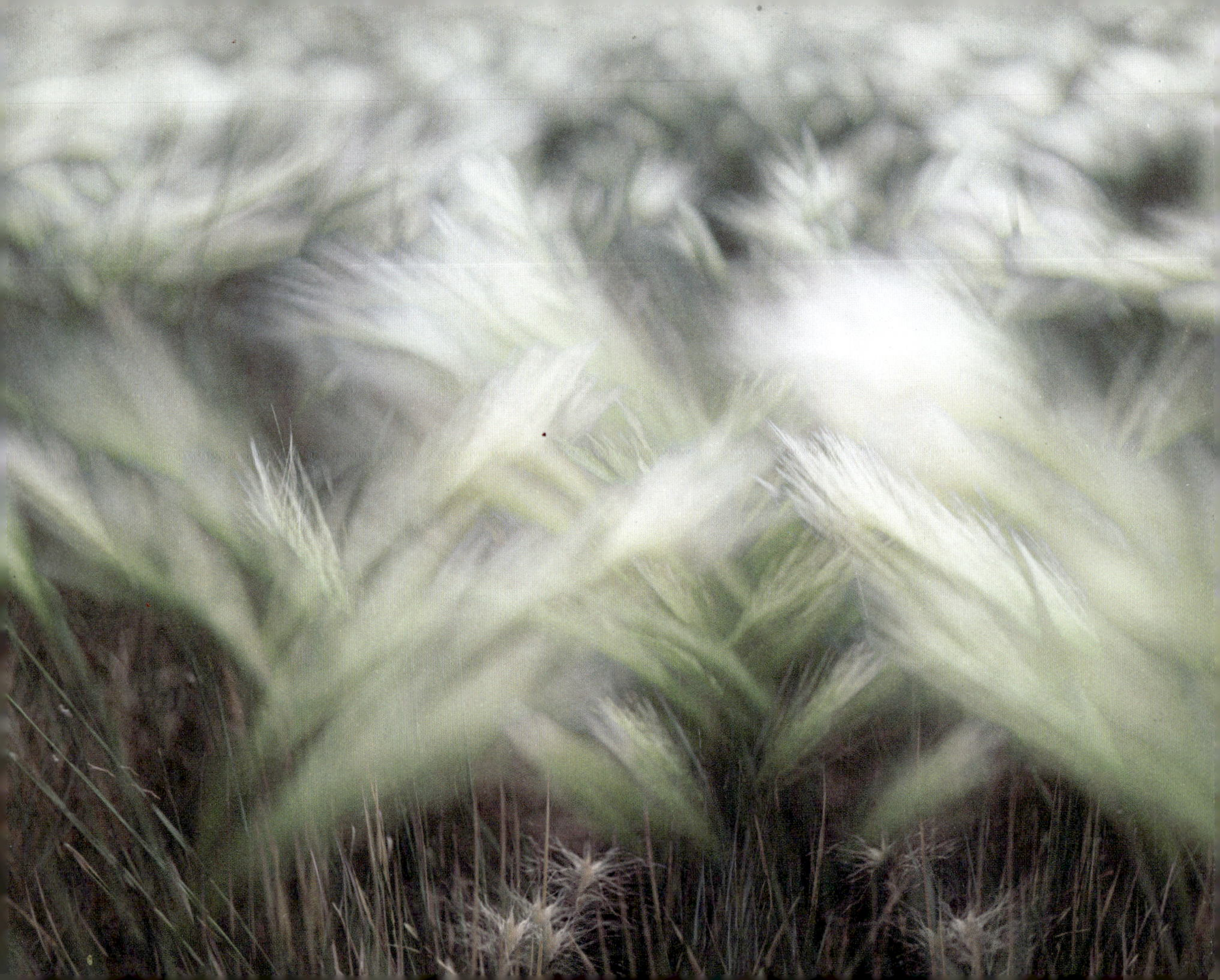